THEY ALSO SERVE

WHO STAND AND WAIT

BY THE SAME AUTHORS

Somewhere in the Midlands
A History of USAAF Station 522 Smethwick.
Brewin Books, 1998

Letters For Victory
History of the First Base Post Office,
Sutton Coldfield, Warwickshire,
during World War II.
Brewin Books, 1993

THEY ALSO SERVE
WHO STAND AND WAIT

FRAN & MARTIN COLLINS

Best wishes

and Fran

Access to Archival
Database (AAD)

Brewin Books

Published by Brewin Books Ltd
Studley, Warwickshire B80 7LG in 2001
www.brewinbooks.com

ISBN 1 85858 204 0

British Library Cataloguing in Publication Data
A Catalogue record for this book is available from the British Library.

Printed and Bound by
Warwick Printing Company Limited,
Theatre Street, Warwick, Warwickshire, CV34 4DR

CONTENTS

FOREWORD

When the first sod was ceremonially cut on 13th June 1937 little thought was given to the impending war in Europe, or the effect it would have on the Pheasey Farms Housing Development. Many Birmingham families were anxiously awaiting word of the completion of their homes and some were already settled in by September 1939 and so evaded the bombings of Birmingham that followed. The quiet and peaceful enjoyment usually granted in real estate lettings was short lived as many of the uncompleted houses were taken over by British forces evacuated from Dunkirk.

In 1942 these houses were let to the 'Army of the United States' to accommodate the overflow of Replacement forces from the 10th Replacement Depot at Lichfield.

To this day few American veterans who served in England at the time are familiar with the name 'Pheasey Farms', or are aware of the important part it played as an army camp for replacement soldiers awaiting assignment to front line units in France. The likelihood is that many English people are unaware of the contribution 'Pheasey Farms' made to the World War II effort.

The American replacements weren't the vast forces of history or legendary warriors, they weren't even all combat soldiers. They were very young ordinary people who befriended the English people of the Pheasey Farms area and shared with them, laughed with them and, in some cases probably cried with them. Many are the heroes buried in the cemeteries of Europe.

So, let's take a long look at 'Pheasey Farms', and let this be notice to the world that Pheasey Farms, a present day residential community, the way it was originally intended, at another time, when the western world was in danger, served as a base for some of the troops that helped defeat Nazism and the Thousand Year Reich

Thomas J. Morrissey - an infantry replacement out of Pheasey Farms 1944.

PREFACE

In 1557 Simon Veysie bought a piece of land in Great Barr for the grand sum of £80. It was he who gave his name to the land which eventually became known as Pheasey Farms.

By the 1930's the land was owned by George Smith. His family had farmed in Great Barr for several generations. He had served for many years on the executive committee of the county branch of the National Farmer's Union and was its President in 1924. In 1935 Mr. Smith sold the land for £32,500 to the First National Housing Trust , a subsidiary of Henry Boot and Sons, while he farmed the neighbouring Park Farm (once the home farm of Great Barr Hall).

By this time the Trust had built 9,300 houses on housing estates around the area of North Birmingham. There was a demand for housing in the suburbs in the 1930's as many people were eager to move out of the overcrowded inner city. Birmingham was in the midst of a building boom.

The Pheasey Estate, which covered 340 acres, was to be a model housing estate. The Trust planned to have sites for all amenities such as shops, churches, public houses and a clinic. Staffordshire Education Committee took 17 acres for the construction of schools. It was intended that more than 3,000 houses should be built on the land.

On 13th July 1937 Sir Kingsley Wood, the then Minister of Health, cut the first sod on the land. Mr.C.Boot (chairman of the Trust) told the minister that:
"In a very short time you will see this landscape covered by houses for the people who are now awaiting them." *
The reporter for the Express and Star confirmed that:
"The first houses will be ready in six months and the entire scheme will be completed in three years." *
However, little did he know that forthcoming world events were soon to curtail the present building boom and it would be a decade before the completed Pheasey Farms Housing Estate would be fully tenanted by the citizens of Birmingham.

Express and Star 13/7/37.

CHAPTER 1
12s.6d. a week

The houses on the Pheasey Estate were to be of the 'working class type'. Some were semi-detached, others were terraced in groups of four or six, all had front and back gardens. Each house was to have three bedrooms and an upstairs bathroom, downstairs there would be a living room and a kitchen. The kitchen contained a sink, gas cooker and a washboiler.

The houses were built specifically for rent which was to range from twelve shillings and six pence to fourteen shillings per week. Three rent collectors were employed by the National Housing Trust to collect the rent, it was also their duty to inform the Trust of any maintenance problems the tenants may have.

To apply to rent one of the Pheasey houses it was necessary to visit Miss Nellie Smith. Originally her office was in the 'White House' on the newly built Beeches Estate, later she used one of the new houses in Beacon Road. Her job was to 'vet' prospective tenants for their 'suitability' and not everyone who went to see her was put on the waiting list. If someone wanted to exchange another National Housing Trust property for one on the Pheasey Estate it was not unknown for her to go and inspect the house the tenant was currently living in to see how they kept it.

At the outbreak of war the building work on the estate was halted. Less than half of the planned houses had been built at this point. Four hundred of the houses were still unoccupied. The Community Centre in Collingwood Drive was unfinished so a large barn, situated behind the Community Centre, was offered to the newly formed Community Association as a temporary building.

As in many new estates roadways, pavements and street lighting were unfinished. Harry Austin moved onto the estate in 1940. He recalls that going out after dark could be hazardous, especially of course in the blackout.

Terry Westwood, whose parents moved into Crome Road sometime in 1940 -'41, remembers that the area looked very different then to the way it does now:

"Beacon Road joined Queslett Road at a simple 'halt' sign by the Old Horns Pub. The shops on the corner of Beacon Road were complete but the shops on the Queslett and Ringinglow Road corner were still being built.- - - Queslett Road itself was a single carriage way and there was a steep embankment from the houses down to the road. Partway up Beacon Road on the left was a CoOp shop with fields around it, there were no other buildings on this side of the road. On the Collingwood Drive and Queslett Road corner stood a tin building known as 'Claire's Hut' where newspapers etc. were sold. The top end of Crome Road ended at an old pig farm (now Farrier Road) and the farmer was called 'Clarkie'. He lived in an old hut known as 'Clarkie's Hut'. On the left of this hut was a very old building known as 'The Library'.

"On the very corner of Tynedale Crescent and Hillingford Road there were no houses. Every so often a mobile cinema would arrive on the open land. This was a large covered lorry which looked rather like a furniture truck. The tailgate would be lifted exposing a large screen. News and information films would be back projected to anyone who cared to stop and watch. If it rained everyone huddled under the tailgate and I well remember comments from the crowd such as : 'It's all the fault of the Boche', or more usually: 'It's all that b—— Hitler's doing.'"

Olive White moved to Pheasey in June of 1939 with her husband and two year old son, Terry. Roland White was a plasterer and was working on the estate at the time. This gave the family precedence when applying for a house.

Alfred and Phyllis Baker moved into Raeburn Road from Smethwick at the onset of war. The houses on the one side of the road backed onto a large field of rough grassland which had been set aside for the school to be built on. Bordering the field were other roads with houses in various stages of development. These houses remained unoccupied when they were completed and eventually were requisitioned by the British Government for British troops.

Mr. and Mrs. Cornforth moved onto the estate in 1941. They had been living in Handsworth but their house suffered bomb damage when a land mine was dropped in nearby James Street and blew their doors and windows in. A kind friend from

TRAINING PIONEERS TO FIGHT

Instruction in firing . grenades from a rifle being given to Pioneers at a Midland camp. (See article on this page.)

..inister of Health (Sir Kingsley Wood) cutting the first .. the Pheasey Estate, Great Barr, to-day, where 3,246 are to be built. On the left is Mr. Charles Boot (chair- ..f the builders) and on the right Mr. Edward Boot (director). Story on Page Seven.

Training Pioneers to fight (B'ham Eve Mail)　　　*Cutting the First Sod (Express and Star)*

2

Collingwood Centre (Edward Atkinson)

Pheasey Farm c.1930's (Kingstanding Library)

Moreland Road offered them a few nights sleeping in her house as a respite from the bombing that was being inflicted on the centre of Birmingham. The Cornforths liked it so much that they went straight away to see Miss Smith to put their names down on the waiting list. At this point the houses in Rippingille Road petered out halfway up. From here there were fields stretching as far as Barr Beacon. There were no houses on the right hand side of Rippingille. Wimperis Way was just a track leading from Beacon Road.

Raymond Smith recalls that he and his family moved to Pheasey from Lozells within a few weeks of the beginning of the war. He remembers moving into 5, Collingwood Drive as winter was approaching. As a 'town boy' he remembers being amazed by a snowstorm that the area suffered one Sunday. He decided to walk in the snow along Collingwood Drive to Beacon Road, up onto Barr Beacon and back via Bridle Lane, Doe Bank Lane and Queslett Road. He reminisces that it was:

"- quite an effort in the snowbanks but a memorable one for a town boy."

Raymond recalls that soon after this it was necessary for he and his family to move to 91, Tynedale Crescent in order to make room for remnants of the British Expeditionary Force that had been evacuated from Dunkirk. He remembers seeing the soldiers, most were without rifles and many even without uniforms. He recalls:

"The first that I encountered was a sergeant who had an army blanket wrapped around his body under his greatcoat, which he tried to sell me! Fortunately there were not many like that!"

Houses to Let Pheasey Estate c.1930's (Kingstanding Library)

NEW TOWN TO BE BUILT HERE.

'New Town To Be Built Here' Pheasey Farms 1937 (Express and Star)

A HOUSING ESTATE IN THE MAKING.

Work is now in full swing—especially for the excavators and levellers—on the new Pheasey Estate, Queslett. The photograph shows workmen completing the first great trench. The First National Housing Trust is going to erect several thousand houses of the middle-class type.

'A Housing Estate In The Making' (Express and Star)

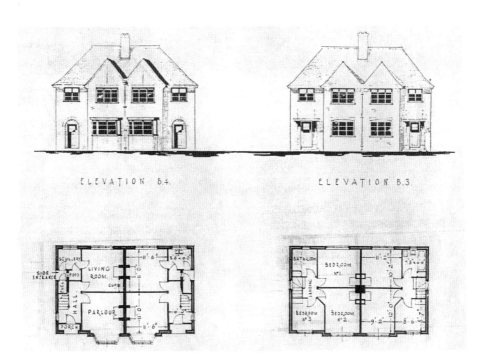

Example of house types on the Pheasey Estate (Walsall Local History Centre)

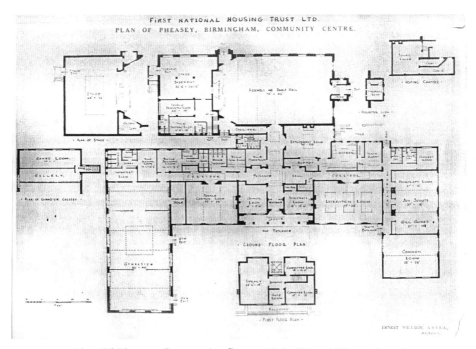

Plan Of Pheasey Community Centre (Walsall Local History Centre)

Occupants were moved out of some of the houses so that the men could be kept together in one area. After this the buildings were used to house the King's Own Royal Regiment and the area was turned into a Pioneer Corps training camp. In the words of the Evening Mail Pheasey became a 'miniature Aldershot'* where military training in firearms, drill and gas mask use was carried out. A unit of the A.T.S. also spent some time at Pheasey during the early stages of the war. At one point a military hospital was based in one of the blocks of houses in Queslett Road. The interior walls between these houses were knocked through to create wards.

In December 1941 events at Pearl Harbour caused America to become involved in the war and early in 1942 plans were made for 'Operation Bolero'+. This was the code name to describe the process of transferring U.S. military forces from the U.S. to the U.K. The U.K. would then become a staging post for an attack on the Axis forces in Europe. The half-finished housing estate at Pheasey Farms was about to play a significant part in this operation.

* Birmingham Mail 20/3/42.
+ This term was borrowed from the composer Maurice Ravel.

CHAPTER 2
Pheasey Farms, Central District, Western Base Section

For the purposes of administration the U.S. military had divided Great Britain into five sections. These were Western, Eastern, Southern, Central and Northern Ireland Base Sections. The Western Base Section, which Pheasey was situated in, stretched from the River Severn right up the middle of the country and included the whole of Wales and Scotland. It had its main headquarters in Chester. From the latter part of 1942 Pheasey's role was as a staging camp within the Western Base Section for units arriving from the States.

The first contingent of Americans to be based at Pheasey arrived in November 1942. Charles Hinde was in this initial group. He had come to England in October 1942 on the Queen Elizabeth. He remembers that there were 18,000 men on board a liner designed to carry 15,000. To accommodate the number of men it was necessary for the ship to be adapted. Most bunks were given five tiers instead of the usual two.

Charles recalls:

"Fortunately my group was among the first to board the ship and we were directed to go to the very top deck (the sundeck)"

Here the bunks had only two tiers as the ceiling was not high enough to accommodate more.

Charles' first assignment was at Whittington Barracks where he performed clerical duties. Charles remembers an officer from Whittington asking him to go to 'Pheasey Farms near Sutton Coldfield' (which he misheard as 'Coalfield'). He was told that he was needed there as a clerk for just one day. Following his orders he drove by truck to Pheasey following behind an officer in a jeep. He remembers looking around for a farm and also a coal mining area, as he says:

"You can imagine my surprise when he (the officer) drove up in front of the present Collingwood Community Centre."

Charles recalls that only a small number of soldiers (about a hundred) were based at Pheasey early in the war. The Collingwood Centre was used as an administration building. There were two clerks working with Charles in his office plus a staff of about eight at the officer's mess hall which was based in the same building.

Charles remembers that after spending the day at Pheasey he was asked to report to the Commanding Officer, Colonel Herr, as the colonel was considering retaining Charles as a clerk at the Collingwood Centre. Charles recalls that:

"I endeavoured to give all pertinent information about myself for I really wanted the job then.. I can remember him saying: 'He is just the man we want' which was music to my ears."

Instead of the one day Charles expected to spend at Pheasey he was stationed there for one year less ten days. Charles was assigned to Headquarters XVIII, Central District, Western Base Section. This unit had jurisdiction over Services of Supply troops* who were responsible for equipping the U.S army in Britain.

Shortly after Charles' arrival at Pheasey he was asked to drive a truck to meet a group of medical personnel, including about 30 nurses, at Snowhill Station in Birmingham for transportation to Pheasey. He remembers:

"I followed an officer driving a jeep and another soldier followed me in another truck. On the return journey darkness and heavy fog soon became a problem, and I soon lost sight of the officer driving the jeep. I was lost, and so was the soldier behind me. I stopped and asked directions five or six times. Finally I observed the cinema on the junction of Walsall Road and Queslett Road, and then I knew the way to Pheasey. But on Queslett Road , near the hospital the fog was so heavy that I simply could not drive in the blackout and the dense fog. The officer who was riding in the cab with me, a medical doctor, got out of the vehicle and walked in front of the truck holding a flashlight. It took about four hours for the return to Pheasey from Snowhill."

Lot Broaddus, a corporal in the medical corps (289th General Hospital) was amongst the personnel travelling to Pheasey. In 1945 he recorded his memories of Pheasey:

"Birmingham is the Detroit of England, and in this vast and scattered metropolis we stayed only a fortnight. We were stationed in a district called Pheasey Farm Estate where we were quartered in two storey brick buildings which were only partially completed. There were British troops stationed at the same place so on the first night we joined up with them and visited the local 'pub' the Trees. We drank bitter ale and beer which, though much different from American beers was quite good. We sang English folk songs with the Tommies and they in turn sang some American ditties with us."+

This group of medical personnel were part of a hospital unit which was composed

Charles Hinde outside the Collingwood Centre

+ *History of Frenchay Hospital - Dr James C. Briggs * See Abbreviations and Terms.*

of nurses, doctors and support staff. The unit was eventually destined to serve in Normandy, landing on Omaha Beach on 16th July 1944. The nurses were billeted at the top of Raeburn Road and in Moreland Road and were probably the only American women to be billeted on the estate. Bob Adams remembers that there was fencing around their quarters to keep them separate from the men billeted on the estate. He also remembers that they didn't make use of the blackout curtains at night. Apparently local Air Raid Wardens became very frustrated with them as they often had the lights on at night. The A.R.P. were convinced that the German bombers could see the lights in their houses. Some of the nurses were billeted in private homes with families. The family were paid sixteen shillings a week to provide meals and a bed for them.

At the beginning of June 1943 the 769th Military Police Battalion arrived at Pheasey Farms. They had sailed from Jersey City on the Queen Elizabeth on May 27th. On June 2nd the group, which consisted of a Headquarters and headquarters detachment and four companies designated the letters A, B, C, and D, disembarked at Greenock and boarded trains to Pheasey Farms which the unit historian described as being:

" - - - near the Pittsburgh of England, Birmingham." *

After orientation lectures and other acclimatisation assignments under the direction of Colonel Herr the Battalion was dispersed: A. Company remained at Pheasey; B.Company went to Cardiff; C.Company went to Liverpool; D.Company

Cooks at Collingwood

Charles Hinde

Unit History of 769th M.P. Battalion.

Pheasey Estate and surrounding area (10th Replacement Depot Archives)

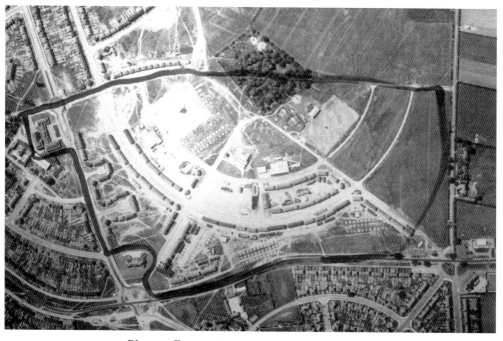

Pheasey Estate (10th Replacement Depot Archives)

went to the Southern Base Section but was later withdrawn and reassigned to Western Base Section when it moved its headquarters to Wem; while the Headquarters and headquarters detachment were moved to Chester.

Company A remained in its original assignment, policing the city of Birmingham and its vicinity. It's H.Q. was located at Pheasey but the company itself was split up into 22 smaller detachments which were sent out to police the surrounding communities like Malvern, Coventry, Walsall, Stratford on Avon, Wolverhampton, Kidderminster, Bromsgrove, Upton on Severn, Ledbury, Govilon, Abergavenny, Hereford, Moreton on Lugg, Wem, Stockingford, Bedworth and Leamington. The two main duties of the 769th were to patrol the towns and to escort convoys. 1st Lieutenant Giddings, the Adjutant considered that:

*"Town patrols were quite effective and contributed largely to the generally good opinion of the American soldier which the British population, after careful consideration, finally had for the American soldier."**

The M.P.s often had to step in to stop fights in the local pubs around Pheasey. Harry Ashford often saw fights outside pubs in the Kingstanding area. He recalls that it was never long before the military police arrived to the screech of brakes. One particular sergeant stands out in Harry's memory. Harry remembers him as being well in excess of six feet tall and as broad as an ox. He was usually one of the first M.P.s to enter a pub where there was trouble and he would soon emerge with two struggling drunks, each grasped by the scruff of the neck.

The M.P. escorts for military convoys were also effective although there was an unfortunate incident in August 1943 when Corporal Florentino Romero of Detachment B, Company A, was killed in an accident while driving a weapons carrier near Worcester.

In February 1944 new regulations were brought in concerning the M.P. uniform. The unit historian records that:

*"The new garb consisted of white helmet liners with the letters M.P. painted in black, white pistol belts, white leggings and wherever possible white gloves."**

He also states that:

*"The procurement of needed materials for whitening was impossible through ordinary channels in sufficient quantity to produce the required results. The officers and men of the Battalion personally purchased the materials needed to bring the Battalion's appearance up to the pronounced wishes of higher command."**

According to the historian:

*"Our outfit becomes very snappy looking when we go into white helmets with the black M.P. painted on front, with pistol belts and white leggings. When we wear white gloves with the aforementioned articles we really stand out in the blackout. Until the townspeople get used to these outfits they are a bit startled by the appearance of our men. This eye arresting get up attracts much attention from the staid British civilians and from our own soldiers. People stop and stare at our men on duty."**

*Unit History of 769th M.P. Battalion.

"OUR JOB"
in the
CORPS OF MILITARY POLICE

M aintaining order, with firmness, fairness and no favoritism.

I nternal security by practicing eternal vigilance.

L iaison with civil authority and maintenance of proper contacts.

I nvestigations, complete, concise, and comprehensive.

T raffic control in assigned area in accord with command requirements.

A rrest of military offenders of all types.

R iot duty, when called on, effectively employed.

Y our government protected, First, Last and Always.

P roperly, courteously and firmly policing all areas.

O rders of the commander enforced by education in preference to arrests.

L and, warfare in all phases when necessary.

I ntelligent service to the command at all times and on all assignments.

C onvoying troops with minimum travel, delay, or friction.

E scorts of all types from Generals to General Prison.

769th MILITARY POLICE BATTALION (ZI)

History of the 769th MP Btn

Nicknames for the M.P.s in their novel uniforms were soon going the rounds. They were called 'Snowdrops', 'Ike's Snowballs' and 'Men in White'. Even the British press commented on the uniforms in editorials and articles with photos.

According to Lieutenant Giddings:

"The white additions to our uniforms were an improvement in two ways. Our men looked neater than ever and during the blackout could be found easily when needed." *

A third advantage , not mentioned by Lieutenant Giddings, to the G.Is who wished to avoid the M.P.s, was that they could now be more easily spotted.

In April 1944 the 17th Base Post Office, known as the 'Invasion Post Office' arrived at Pheasey. The men of this unit were to spend several months working alongside the 1st Base Post Office in Sutton Coldfield which was processing mail for the troops in the United Kingdom. The unit was to travel to France shortly after D-Day to serve the troops on the Continent.

After sailing to England on the 'Ile de France', a former luxury liner, the men travelled by train on the L.M.S. Railway to Lichfield where they learnt they were to sleep in 'pyramidals' (tents) at South Camp, which was situated about a mile away from the main buildings at Whittington Barracks. James Brady remembers the bus ride from there to Pheasey:

"Spirits were indeed at their highest peak yet attained among the crowds of us as we anxiously awaited the end of our bus jaunt from South Camp to Pheasey Farms. Unrestrained voices rang out in song as the squeaking buses slid around the wide

Operations and Co-ordinating Section. Pheasey Billeting Arrangement (10th Replacement Depot Archives)

* *Unit History of 769th M.P. Battalion.*

corner past a large pub and up the main street of Pheasey.

"*One block-long cluster after another of stone houses flanked the roads as we surged into the camp proper. All of a sudden we came upon a group of pyramidals in a large area of dirt and mud. Much to our chagrin the pulls of the engine seemed to lessen in intensity as we neared the tent compound.*

"*'Omigawd!' 'No, it can't be. They told us we were gonna live in real houses with roofs over our heads.' 'I'll never believe another thing in the Army as long as I'm in it.'*

"*So flowed the conversation as our grins faded to frowns. For an agonising two or three minutes we waited, prayerfully urging the bus driver to keep his foot on the gas and make tracks out of this forlorn area.*

"*The sigh of relief that went through the bus as we gradually pulled out of sight of those tents must have been audible for blocks. It was like that of a condemned man who receives a full pardon a moment before he is to sit in the electric chair. At last we rounded the last corner and made a complete stop in front of a series of two storey red brick buildings.*"*

The aforementioned units used the Pheasey Farms Estate as a staging area before moving on, usually to the Continent, but on 1st March 1943 the role of Pheasey as a staging camp changed. As Operation Bolero progressed a network of Replacement Depots came into being across the country and Pheasey Farms became part of the 10th Replacement Depot, as a subdepot to Whittington Barracks in Lichfield.

**The Invasion Post Office.*

CHAPTER 3

Operation Bolero

Whittington Barracks in Lichfield, Staffordshire had been handed over to the U.S. forces in Britain in late 1942, as a staging area for the expected Allied invasion of Europe, or, as some would say, a base for the Allied invasion of Britain, otherwise known as Operation Bolero. On 1st March 1943 the 10th Replacement Depot was activated at Whittington Barracks in the Western Base Section. It's motto was 'Can Do' and its slogan was 'We are not surprised by anything.'

The primary mission of the Replacement Depots was to process casual replacements from the States, Disciplinary Training Centres, General Hospitals or other military organisations, for reassignment. The depot had four main functions. These were to receive, classify, equip and ship out troops arriving for active service in the European Theatre of Operations and later for return to the United States

As the official archives for Whittington Barracks states.

"Through this 10th Replacement Depot, one of the most progressive in England pass W.A.C.s, sailors, Red Cross Women, various Allied officers, male civilians, male and female civil service workers, aswell as hundreds of thousands of American officers and enlisted men for processing and routing each day. All must be fed, equipped, housed, paid, entertained and transported, given pills and medical attention, when sick and dental care when necessary, given glasses if needed and placed at their proper post. Here at the depot the numerous wounds of battle are treated and new strength supplied to the armies in the field. In modern warfare the outcome of battles often hinges on the speed with which replacements and reinforcements are brought to the front."*

1st Lieutenant Martin T. Anderson, the unit historian of the 49th Reinforcement Battalion, which was based at Pheasey, felt that his unit's task was:

" To furnish the Field Forces and the Services of Supply reinforcements in the desired specification at the time and place directed and in the highest possible state of physical, professional, mental and moral development for combat."*

Four Replacement Battalions played a part in the history of Pheasey Farms as a Replacement Depot substation. All spent some time at Whittington Barracks. The Replacement Battalions operated separately to the M.P. Battalion and the Supply units that were already based at Pheasey.

4th Replacement Battalion

The first Replacement Battalion to arrive at Pheasey was the 4th, which was comprised of four replacement companies designated the letters A, B, C, and D. This

*Military Archives of the 10th Replacement Depot.

unit had been activated at Camp Edwards, Massachusetts, and had left New York Harbor on the Queen Elizabeth on 31st August 1942, destination unknown. After reaching Great Britain the unit travelled to Whittington Barracks arriving there on 7th September 1942. On 18th September 1943 the Battalion, which at the time consisted of 13 officers and 95 enlisted men, entrucked at Whittington Barracks at 1500 hours and arrived at Pheasey Farms Estate at 1530 hours.

The 4th was the chief source of casual replacements required by the U.S.Army Forces in the European Theatre of Operations (excluding the Air Forces). It also supplied large numbers of casual replacements to organisations alerted for service in the African Campaign.

Captain Mortimer Pier and 1st Lieutenant Donald Parks were responsible for supervising the Training Programme for Reinforcements in this battalion. Instruction was given to reinforcements in accordance with the type of organisation to which they would be assigned:

"The subject material stressed in the Ground Force Replacement Command

HQ Det 49th Repl. Bn, Collingwood Centre (Mavis Haase)

Training Memorandum is presented in the form of Lecture Discussion Groups and Practical Work. These methods are augmented by the use of such Training Aids as are obtainable. Each company of the Battalion has been provided with a classroom, the seating capacity of which is 250 men. These classrooms are equipped with blackboards, situation maps and instructional posters." *

At the end of the year the battalion was reorganised to include a medical detachment. This detachment was probably billeted in Eastlake Close. At the beginning of 1944 the replacement companies were redesignated the numbers 293, 294, 295 and 296 to replace the letters A,B,C,and D.

37th Replacement Battalion

On 10th November 1943 B. Company (later to become 302nd Replacement Battalion.) was assigned to Pheasey to assume the duties of Receiving and Shipping. The other three companies of the Battalion remained at Whittington Barracks.

48th Replacement Battalion

The 48th Replacement Battalion, consisting of the 317th, 318th, 319th and 320th Replacement Companies was attached to the 10th Replacement Depot. All the companies except the 320th, who remained at Whittington, spent some time at

321st Reinforcement Room (10th Replacement Depot Archives)

*4th Reinforcement Battalion Archives.

Crest of the 10th Replacement Depot (10th Replacement Depot Archives)

Pheasey during the first few months of 1944.

The 317th, the Headquarters and headquarters detachment, consisting of eleven officers and 161 enlisted men, arrived by truck from Doddington Park, Nantwich, Cheshire at the beginning of January. The unit left on 7th February to spend a month at Arbury park, Nuneaton, carrying out guard duties.

The 318th, consisting of three officers and 458 enlisted men arrived at Pheasey on 29th January from Madeley Tileries, Newcastle Under Lyme by motor transport. The 319th, consisting of two officers and 458 enlisted men arrived at Pheasey from Packington Park, Meriden, Warwickshire on 19th February.

The battalion's stay at Pheasey was short. On 13th April the whole battalion left by rail for South Hill, near Dulveton, Somerset.

49th Replacement Battalion

The 49th Replacement Battalion, consisting of the 321st, 322nd, 323rd, and 324th Replacement Companies also arrived at Pheasey in 1944.

The 322nd arrived on 12th April and became the largest holding of the 10th Replacement Depot. It handled the details for the entire camp in addition to processing and training several hundred casual enlisted men for shipment in the U.K. until D-Day.

On 16th April the 323rd moved to Pheasey to enable Whittington Barracks to billet a large contingent of W.A.C. personnel arriving at the depot. This W.A.C.unit had

322nd Company Orderly Room & Billets (10th Replacement Depot Archives)

come to England to serve at the 1st Base Post Office in Sutton Coldfield to aid the processing of mail for the U.S. troops in the U.K. The 323rd returned to Whittington ten days later.

In May the 321st and Headquarters and headquarters Detachment for the 49th arrived at Pheasey. In August the the 324th arrived at Pheasey.

Once the Replacement Battalions were settled at Pheasey men started arriving at the camp to be processed and then sent to join the combat troops who were training around various parts of England and Wales, or noncombatant troops who were based in the U.K. to supply and support the fighting forces. Generally these troops were unattached to a combat unit prior to arriving at the base. Sidney and Sylvia Barker recall that these G.I.s arrived at Pheasey ' *in a trickle, rather than a flood.*'

Pat Capasso was one of those who did not belong to a regular outfit when he arrived at Pheasey. He came via Whittington Barracks and he recalls that on his arrival he was '*just a scared 19 year old kid in a foreign land.*' Most of the men around him were comparative strangers. He remembers arriving at Pheasey at approximately 3 a.m. in the pitch black and extreme cold.

Pheasey did receive some large contingents of men. One particular group of 600 - 800 men came by train from Gouroch in Scotland on 8th June 1943, having sailed from New York. Alf Lovell was a guard on this train. He remembers receiving orders to go to Carlisle Station to pick up the U.S.troop train, which consisted of ten coaches, a guard van and a Stanier Black Five Engine guard's.

Billets Insignia of the 3rd Infantry Division and 90th Infantry Division (10th Replacement Depot Archives)

The journey from Carlisle to Great Barr Station (now Hamstead Station) took six or seven hours. The train had a temporary halt at Derby where the men were given packed lunches, their first food in Britain.

G.I. Bill Beatty was on that train and wrote down his first impressions of Britain in a letter to his mother:

"We had a long train ride after we landed - - - which was just as interesting as the boat ride. It seems funny to be going through places I read about in history and geography. - - - I am very much impressed with the countryside. Perhaps most noticeable is the similarity of everything all brick houses about the same size and design - every town looked like suburbs of American cities like Northwood in Baltimore for instance, except most of them have red roofs.

Then nearly everywhere are stone fences - some enclosing cows and sheep, but mostly just pastures with no animals. Every home, city or country, seems to have a Victory garden in their back yard. Everybody from kids on up waved at us 'Yanks' and we waved back, especially to the lassies. So far it doesn't seem much more like we are in the real war zone than back home, except in the cities we passed through where Hitler had visited and dropped a few 'eggs'. The industrial and railroad sections seem like ours, with many women working in factories and yards. Very few cars were seen as petrol is as scarce here as our gasoline."

Alf Lovell talked to several of the G.I.s on the long journey. He remembers them

Major Free, C.O. of 4th Reinforcement Battalion (10th Replacement Depot Archives)

323rd Reinforcement Company Orderly room & billet (10th Replacement Depot Archives)

321st Reinforcement Company Orderly room & billets (10th Replacement Depot Archives)

being very curious about the areas they were travelling through. He also remembers them asking him to explain English money to them.

The train arrived at Great Barr Station at about 4a.m. and Alf recalls that it was necessary to put the gas lights on at the station so that the men could see to get off the train As the station platform was not very long Alf remembers that the first six coaches drew level with the platform to let the men off and then the train had to pull forward so that the baggage could be unloaded from the rear four coaches. Alf remembers the officers alighting first, then the enlisted men who were lined up on the platform. They were then given instructions to march over the bridge where British troops would give them further directions. From the bridge the men had to march two miles up to Pheasey, while their bags were transported by truck.

Raymond Smith, a teenager at the time, remembers walking down Hillingford drive from the bus stop at Tyndale crescent at about 11p.m. one night when he met his 'first Americans':

"They were marching up the hill loaded with kit and rifles with two men at the front and rear of the offside rank carrying storm lanterns. There was a strong smell of wet woolen uniforms, and they looked worn out. I think they had probably marched from Hamstead after a long wet journey from the U.S."

Vera Stanley and Olive White remember being woken up as the men marched up to the camp. Vera remembers hearing music in the distance, as it became louder she realised that it was men singing 'The Yanks are Coming' and *"Believe me,"* she says

Pheasey Estate Control Point (10th Replacement Depot Archives)

"they were, hundreds and thousands of them." Olive remembers jeeps and marching feet going up and down Raeburn Road. She reminisces:

"They all seemed so young and so tall and all with different accents."

Bill Beatty recalls his first impressions of Pheasey in the letter to his mother:

"Now I am at another temporary place, expecting to be assigned and moved at any time. We are living in houses - a housing project on the outskirts of a large city, taken over by the army before it was completed. But they're just bare rooms with double bunks, although more homelike than barracks. The chow here is excellent, probably comes from the U.S.A., as it isn't much different. I guess we won't find much different food unless we get into towns away from the camp. It hardly seems possible that we're 3,000 miles from home, as we're carrying on in our own way for the most part. I'm running around tending to my First Sergeant business just as if I were back in the States contacting British and American soldiers and English civilians."

Albert Eisenkraft also made the journey to Great Barr by train. He arrived in 1944. Prior to this he had never travelled far from New York City--

"So being sent all over the U.S.A. and then overseas was quite an experience. We landed at Glasgow and were transported to a waiting train (with doors in the sides which amazed us) and travelled through the night to an unknown destination. It turned out to be Birmingham, and a ride to a suburban development of (to us) pretty classy brick houses - Pheasey Farms."

In November 1943 Fred Petrogallo made a similar journey to Great Barr by train

323rd Reinforcement Company Orderly room and billets (10th Replacement Depot Archives)

although he was lucky enough to be transported by truck from Great Barr Station. At the time the weather was bitterly cold and his first impressions of England were not particularly good. He went into the mess hall when he arrived but there was no change of temperature inside the building. Fred even remembers that the G.I. who was sitting at the piano had his gloves on. The meal of cold toast and coffee, which the men had to stand to eat, was not particularly appetising.

Joyce Ongley, who lived on the Pheasey Estate also recalls how cold the winters were there. She remembers that it was nicknamed 'Little Russia' while Gwen Shelton remembers it being called 'Siberia' because in winter Pheasey was usually blocked with snow from the Queslett Road side. To many of the G.I.s the area became known as 'Freezy Pheasey' or 'Freezy Farms'.

Eighteen year old Earl Lovelace arrived at the camp in December 1943. He recalls: *"The first thing I remember is it was COLD and then it got colder."*

He remembers that shortly after his arrival all in his group except himself and one other man were sent directly to take part in Operation Torch, the invasion of North Africa. He and his colleague were left behind as their records had been lost. They had to wait for them to be found before they could be processed and sent on.

For many G.I.s their first impressions of Pheasey were not positive. They had come to fight a war against the Axis forces in Europe that posed little threat to their own homeland. They were miles away from home with no prospect of seeing their loved ones for several months or even years, if at all. They were cold, tired and hungry, many of them had travelled directly from Glasgow and had had very little rest. Even so Pheasey, with its brick built buildings was a more attractive prospect than the tented camps that they may have been sent to.

CHAPTER 4
Guard Duty

James Brady of the 17th B.P.O. remembers his delight on arrival at Pheasey to find that he and his unit were to be billeted in brick buildings instead of tents. But his delight was short-lived when he noticed the eight foot high security fence topped with barbed wire that surrounded the camp. He recalls the initial comments made while the men of the 17th B.P.O. were still on the bus.

"'Hey bud, you stopped at the wrong place.' 'What's that wire fence doing there?' 'I thought the guard house was over in Lichfield.' 'Brother, it looks as though we done had it. Guess we're gonna be quarantined for a while.'

"For true enough, an eye opening, spirit dampening wire fence was strung menacingly in front of a whole block of our new billets. We didn't know if it was erected to keep the civilians out or us in." *

The fence effectively created a compound to segregate the part of the estate that was occupied by the military from the civilian housing. Several people remember the fence being erected at the rear of their own houses. The military part of the estate was normally off limits to civilians unless they were part of the local service industries or roundsmen. Civilians who lived on the estate needed an I.D. card to come and go, especially at night time. As time went on Jean Phillips remembers that it became unnecessary to show the pass.

James Brady recalls the talk that he and the men of the 17th B.P.O. were given by the C.O. when they arrived at Pheasey:

"The Colonel, in his first talk, laid down the law to us. 'The sidewalk in front of your billets is your boundary line,' he told us. 'One foot off the curb and you're out of bounds. See those houses up there? (pointing to a row of houses that sat right off the edge of our section). 'Look at them but don't go in them. They are private homes and you will not enter any private homes.'" *

A curfew was imposed on G.I.s who wished to go off camp limits. This was, of course, highly unpopular. It was not only unpopular with the G.I.s themselves who would be limited by it but also with the officers and men who had to enforce it.

The casual replacements at Pheasey took turns to be on guard duty. G.I. Tom Morrissey remembers that this was not a popular task for the men:

"The most difficult part of guard duty was the night tour which consisted of two hours on and two hours off for sleep. I could never will myself to sleep by the clock and the guard house was usually noisy."

Tom remembers that Saturday night was the busiest when many late stragglers tried to sneak over the fence. He recalls:

"Most of the casual guards would let the delinquents go if the coast was clear, and

*Invasion Post Office -James Brady.

if it wasn't the corporal of the guard could determine whether it was safe or not to take a late comer back to his billet. We protected each other whenever possible."

Tom, who also carried out guard duty at Whittington Barracks, believes that Pheasey was more relaxed than Whittington (known to some G.I.s as Stalag Lichfield) from where the tales of brutality to prisoners led to the trial of Colonel Kilian (C.O.) at the end of the war. Kilean appears to have been generally unpopular with the enlisted men. Charles Hinde remembers hearing that he had once been attacked by a soldier as his car made the turn at The Trees to enter the Pheasey area. There are similar stories about him being attacked in the area around Whittington Barracks.

The guards at Whittington were issued with live ammunition (while the guards at Pheasey were not) and while there Tom remembers being ordered to shoot at any part of the prisoner that appeared out of the windows of the cells. (Bullet holes in the walls around the windows of the guard house bear testimony to this.) Tom was relieved to see that the guard houses at Pheasey did not have any windows.

The Walsall Observer relates an incident when a Walsall girl ended up in court as a consequence of attempting to return a G.I. to Pheasey before the curfew. Apparently 37 year old Nora Anderson's boss had allowed her to borrow the firm's van to get home from work on Christmas Day and return on December 27th. This was on the understanding that the van would be garaged at Ward's Farm at Goscote on Boxing Day.

MP on duty at Entrance to Pheasey on Romney Way (10th Replacement Depot Archives)

Nora had been entertaining a G.I. from Pheasey at her home on the 26th. At 10 p.m. she realised that if he caught the bus he would not be able to get back to the base before the curfew, so she decided to use the van to drive him as far as Park Hall. As she returned up the Broadway two police officers signalled her to stop by flashing red lights. She slowed up but then gathered speed. Unfortunately for her, as the van passed the policemen they noted the firm's name on its side and were able to trace her as being the driver.

She was charged with taking and driving a motor van without consent, driving it without insurance, wasting petrol and failing to stop at the request of the police. In her defence her solicitor, Mr.Charles Hodgkinson, submitted that:

" - there could be no conviction on the first summons as the van was in the defendant's possession at the time with the consent of the owner and if she was not guilty of that offence she could not be guilty of the second as the insurance policy would still be in force. She admitted wasting the small quantity of petrol required to drive from Goscote to Park Hall and back but if she had not done so the American soldier would have got into trouble and she only took him the shortest possible distance."*

In her defence Nora also stated that she did not see the policemen signalling her to stop:

"She noticed two red lights in the road but thought they were intended as a warning for her to slow around the island at the junction. She did not see any policemen and did not know that she was called upon to stop."*

Nora lost her job as a consequence of using the van without permission but by the time the case came to court she had another driving job. Mr. Hodgkinson stated that:

"In view of the difficulty of obtaining motor drivers it would be against the national interests if her licence were suspended"*

Superintendent Raybould decided that charges wouldn't be pressed against her for failing to stop and the magistrates decided that she was not guilty of taking the van without consent. She was fined one pound for not having an insurance policy and two pounds for wasting petrol but it was decided that her licence shouldn't be endorsed as far as the driving of commercial vehicles was concerned.

Generally the G.I.s at Pheasey seemed undeterred by the curfew and would regularly return late. Many devised ways of getting back to their billets without encountering the guards or M.P.s. Albert Eisenkraft would regularly miss the last bus back to Pheasey when visiting his girlfriend in Handsworth. He would walk the five miles back to Pheasey-:

"- - listening carefully for the sounds of M.P. jeep motors. Fortunately the houses along my road home had thick hedges on their fronts. I hid in these as soon as a motor sound came my way. The M.P.s at Pheasey were a problem but at the time there was a large open field in front of the development. I crawled the last several hundred yards over that field and had plenty of fellow infiltraters. It being after 11p.m. the M.P.

Walsall Observer.

vigilance was low. Looking back, maybe they didn't try too hard."

Resident, Steve Smith, remembers that those who caught buses back to the base after the curfew would often alight from the buses before they got to the camp gates. They would then hide behind hedges before creeping through the back gardens of the civilian houses on the estate.

They would use the same procedure for getting out of the camp when they did not have a pass. Olive White remembers G.I.s getting out through the school gates in Raeburn Road. They would then proceed across the road, down the side of Olive's house (number 8) and out of bounds into Collingwood Road. Her son, Terry, recalls:

"One night my father heard our back gate open and close. He ran to the door in time to see two G.I.s going down our garden path. He called out: 'What do you think you are doing?' They said they were trying to get across to Collingwood Drive to dodge the M.P. patrol. My father told them to carry on and it became a regular occurrence."

Bob Adams was not so happy about the G.I.s using his garden as a shortcut. He had already told some of the G.I.s he knew that they should always ask first before using someone's garden as a right of way, so he and his wife, Dorothy were surprised one evening to hear a commotion in their garden. The couple had already retired to bed when they heard an assortment of American voices shouting and cursing accompanied

MP on duty at Entrance to Pheasey on Doe Bank Lane (10th Replacement Depot Archives)

by the barking of Bob's mongrel dog, Bruce.

As Bob rushed downstairs he saw several figures disappearing over the bottom of his garden. One of them was straddled across the fence uttering profanities but unable to move as Bob's dog was attached to his leg. In turn the dog was attached to the kennel which he had dragged by his chain right up the garden. It was necessary for Bob, who had had St. John Ambulance training to disengage the dog from the G.I. and treat the man's wound. Needless to say the Adams didn't get American intruders in their garden again.

Edna Puttergill was also unhappy about the G.I.s using her garden as a shortcut. Many soldiers were the worse for drink when trying to sneak back to their billets and therefore were not particularly quiet or careful while stumbling across people's gardens in the semi darkness, trampling on flower beds and leaving gates open.

Edna's husband, Frank, was away from home serving with the R.A.F. and she felt quite vulnerable, especially at night. She was often disturbed by G.I.s cutting through her garden, and on one occasion she remembers hearing a shot although she was too frightened to see what was happening. Eventually she and her neighbour, Mrs. Mullings, decided to report the problem to the M.P.s in the guard room in Romney Way. Both refused to give their name and address when making the complaint for fear of reprisals, but action was taken and her garden ceased being a shortcut.

MP on duty HQ Building (10th Replacement Depot Archives)

Shortly after the complaint Bob Webb remembers an officious looking M.P. cradling a carbine in his arms, knocking at his door and speaking to his father. Bob remembers the man assuring his father that the M.P.s would be patrolling the area and that they would ensure that G.I.s would not be taking shortcuts through the gardens from this time on.

G.I. John Carpenter was often late back to camp after visiting his girlfriend, Rose Wright, whose father's land bordered the northern perimeter of the camp. The six foot high spiked railings on this side of the camp had been erected some years earlier as a boundary to the farmland but were now utilised by the military to form part of the security fencing. Jim, Rose's brother, would often assist John to clear the railings so that he could get back to his billet undetected by the guard who would stand at the entrance to the camp on the corner of Doe Bank Road and Stanhope Way. If the guards were in the vicinity patrolling the camp boundary Jim would approach the fence on his own and engage the guard in conversation while John walked a little further on and scrambled over the fence while the guard's attention was diverted.

John remembers that the M.P.s who had jeeps would often park them on the Southern face of Barr Beacon during the day from where they could scan the perimeter of the camp using binoculars. When a G.I. was spotted climbing over the boundary fence the M.P.s could race to the area in their jeeps in order to arrest the man. Terry Westwood remembers seeing jeeps driving slowly around the estate at night. Each jeep carried four M.P.s wearing their distinct white helmets.

Mrs. Procter recalls that if the men jumped camp to go for a beer the M.P.s would go after them in the jeeps, hitting them with their nightsticks when they were caught then throwing them into the back of their jeeps. Edward Holmes remembers the M.P.s patrolling Walsall in their jeeps. He also remembers the occasion when they fired at a group of deserters in Park Street.

John Carpenter recalls:

"A lot of guys from the camp used to go A.W.O.L. so the M.P.s used to carry out random checks on local farms and outbuildings to flush out any G.I.s who might be hiding there."

Doe Bank farm, where John and Mary Pickering lived and worked lay across the road from one of the entrances to the camp. From time to time the Pickerings would find U.S. Army blankets or overcoats lying in the hay in their barn, although they never saw the men themselves.

Sixteen year old Harry Ashford, who used to work as a labourer on Wrights Farm, remembers a dirty, unshaven and generally dishevelled G.I. approach him one day to ask him the way to Birmingham, avoiding the main thoroughfares of Pheasey, which Harry was happy to do. On another occasion while Harry was labouring for farmer George Smith, he encountered a G.I. in a distraught condition who asked for directions across the fields to Walsall to avoid any patrolling M.P.s Harry directed him through St. Margaret's Wood to Chapel Lane and the A34. Sometime later Harry was approached by M.P.s who informed him that they were looking for a G.I. who had stabbed a fellow soldier. Having no desire to get involved further Harry pleaded ignorance.

Sometimes when John Carpenter visited Rose Wright he would dress in 'civvies' as a farm worker. The M.P.s often visited the farm while John was dressed in this way but never recognised him.

Other G.I.s acquired civilian clothing so that they could move freely outside the camp without detection by the M.P.s. Some were caught in cafes and eating places where they gave themselves away with their American style of eating, using only a fork. To ensure that this didn't happen to him John comments:

"I learnt to eat English style pretty damn quick."

The punishment for being caught out after curfew was to be locked up in one of the guard houses at Pheasey. This would be followed by a court martial at Whittington Barracks where the accused would usually be sentenced to six months hard labour less two thirds pay. This was known as 'six months parade and rest'. Lesser crimes were punished by the offender being placed on fatigue duties or K.P.

Irene Lang (nee Smith) remembers the occasion that her fiance, Bill, attended a family party at her house. Bill was enjoying the party and was loath to leave early to get back to camp so he decided to concoct an excuse for not returning. The following day two M.P.s called at Irene's house to enquire why Bill had not returned to camp. Bill told the M.P.s that he was unwell and was suffering from gastroenteritis.

MP standing guard across the road from the Collingwood Centre. 1943 (C. Hinde)

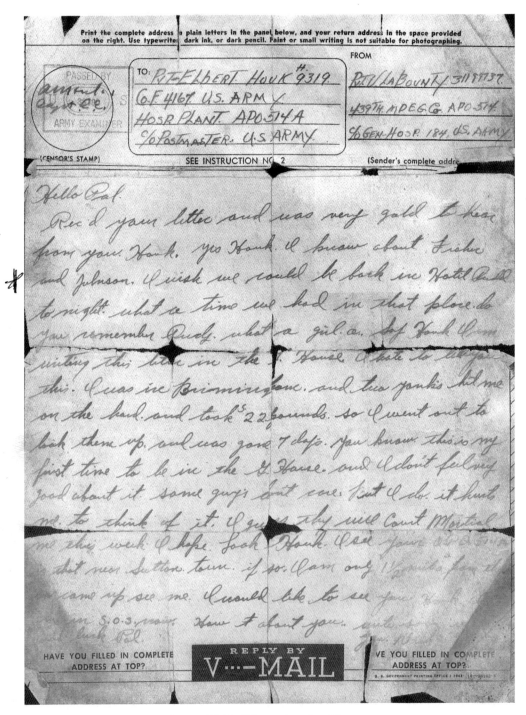

Copy of V. Mail letter found at Pheasey

Nevertheless the M.P.s took Bill to Whittington barracks where he was confined to sick quarters and put on a starvation diet for two days.This certainly cured Bill's illness and he didn't suffer from that complaint again.

Irene remembers that Bill did manage to get away from camp fairly regularly as his platoon sergeant, who was a close friend of his, allowed him to fill in his own pass out which he would then sign. Albert Eisenkraft remembers that passes for going off base were difficult to obtain but could be acquired by slipping the sergeant five dollars. Albert didn't find this practice acceptable so his nightly jaunts were, as he puts it, 'illegal'.

Recently a letter was found in one of the lofts of the houses on the Pheasey Estate. It is thought to have been sent by a G.I. who spent some time in the guard house at Pheasey. Private V.LaBounty writes concerning his feelings about spending time in the guard house:

"I'm writing this letter in the G.House. I hate to tell you this. I was in Birmingham and two Yanks hit me on the head and took 22 pounds. So I went to look them up and was gone seven days. You know this is my first time to be in the G.House and I don't feel very good about it. Some guys don't care but I do. It hurts me to think of it. I guess they will court martial me this week."

The guardhouses at Pheasey were located in the first two houses of Romney Way where there was also a sentry box and a barrier across the road. There was another entrance to the camp on the corner of Stanhope Way and Doe Bank Road where there was a barrier and sentry box. The final entrance to the camp was at the top of Raeburn Road where there were gates onto the camp which were patrolled by guards. The gates into the school in Raeburn Road also led onto parts of the camp. The guard house for this part of the estate was 11, Moreland Road.

On cold winter nights Sidney and Sylvia Barker would take hot coffee to the armed guards who used to stand in front of number 11. On one occasion, after having taken coffee out to sentry on guard duty Sid noticed a tall, red haired sergeant approaching them. As he approached the guard he remarked to him, 'Just remember soldier, you haven't seen me this evening.' After this he disappeared into a nearby house.

On another occasion Sid was returning home from work one Saturday afternoon, when he was confronted by half a dozen G.I.s running down the drive at the side of his house, coming from the direction of his back garden. Apparently they had escaped from the guardhouse at the bottom of the Barker's garden, cut a hole in the security fencing and ran through the garden.

The Barkers also recall the occasion when they were startled by a loud bang coming from the direction of number 11. The guards had apparently lit a fire in the fireplace, not realising that the water had been turned off to avoid burst pipes during the frosty weather. As there was no water in the back boiler it had exploded.

Vic Tims, a resident on the estate, remembers the occasion that his six year old brother, Richard, ended up in the guard house in Romney Way. Richard, goaded by his friend, was persuaded to crawl under the security fence. As he proceeded to do this he was scared out of his wits by the sound of gunshot above his head. He froze but as he lay there he was grabbed by a guard and hauled off to the guardroom.

Mrs. Tims was furious when her neighbours came to inform her that her young son had nearly been shot. She took Vic by the arm and bundled his baby sister into the pushchair before setting off for the guardroom to give the guards a piece of her mind. Once there she left the G.I.s in no doubt as to how annoyed she was with them. In due course they apologised and released Richard into his mother's care. In order to placate Mrs. Tims the M.P.s and guards concerned put together a large box of goodies which included candy bars, fruit, tinned goods and scented soap. Needless to say this mollified Mrs. Tims who left the guard house in a better temper than when she had entered it.

CHAPTER 5

Half Finished Council Houses

A large part of the estate that had been built by the beginning of the war was used to house American soldiers. The following roads had G.I.s billeted in them: Romney Way; Chantrey Crescent; Raeburn Road; Gainsborough Crescent; Hillingford Avenue; Pomeroy Road; Rippingille Road; Moreland Road; Collingwood Drive; Bramley Close and Eastlake Close.

Most of the houses were in blocks of four or six. There were a number of semidetached with an occasional block of three together. The G.I.s called the larger blocks 'row houses'. The blocks of four and six had passages cut through them to provide an entry to the back garden for the residents. Gordon Baker remembers that these were bricked up to provide extra dormitory room for the men.

Both upstairs and downstairs rooms were used for sleeping quarters. At first the enlisted men slept on the floor, but as numbers increased roughly made bunk beds, which the men called 'double deckers', were fixed into the rooms. As time went on it was necessary for each room to sleep eight to ten enlisted men. Johnnie Alegrezza, who was billeted in Collingwood Drive, recalls that there were 36 men sleeping in his house. John Carpenter remembers that lack of space in the small rooms was a problem. In order to walk between the beds during the day it was necessary to stow all kit and duffel bags on the bed. At night everything had to be replaced on the floor so that the men could get into the beds.

The officers were better off. William Brothers remembers that several of them were billeted in a house, but each had a separate room. Richard Long recalls that there were approximately four officers billeted to each house.

Tom Morrissey remembers that the enlisted men's beds were not particularly comfortable. The tier of the lower bunk was about six inches from the floor while the second tier was about four foot high off the ground. Each tier had baling wire criss-crossed across it to form 'springs'. Three straw pads known as 'biscuits' were placed on the base to make up the 'mattress'. Tom recalls that they were: *"not really conducive to beauty rest or sleep."*

James Brady and the men of the 17th B.P.O. were also dissatisfied with the lack of comfort. He writes:

"Another phase of our Pheasey was the struggle to make our beds more comfortable. It seems that by a stroke of good fortune there was a huge haystack in the field across the street - a wonderful substitute for those inner springs of happier days. It also seems that there was some law or edict against dragging off any section of said hay for any reason whatever, especially for cramming into mattress covers.

"However, before the Colonel had the chance to gather us together for the first of

a series of talks on how to conduct ourselves in our new environment, a parade of fatigue clad huskies was seen lugging the best part of their beds across the field and into their respective billets. In the distance a nonplussed irate farmer stood yelling and ranting about his haystack that had suddenly shrunk to a shadow of its former height.

"When the Colonel managed to get the men together to lay the law down to them he said:

'There is a haystack in the field across the street. You will not take any of that hay for your mattress covers' (much muffled laughter, some not so muffled)."*

James also remembers the sparseness of the rooms:

"The rooms were bare with the exception of the homemade 'double deckers' and perhaps a table and chair. A fireplace and sink in the kitchen though, surpassed our wildest dreams." *

Some G.I.s, like John Carpenter, were not so lucky, and although they had sinks and toilets fitted in their houses they were not connected to mains water so each day it was necessary to trudge to a separate latrines and washhouse.

Many G.I.s were not impressed with their living quarters. David Lampl expresses his feelings about them by stating that the nissen huts just outside Warminster:

" - - - were not as bad as the half finished council houses that were part of the barracks of the replacement depot outside Birmingham where we had to go if we were going to France as individual G.I.s and not as members of units. Rather than sleep in that overpacked filth another G.I. and I once spent half a night walking the streets of

Headquarters Building Collingwood Centre (10th Replacement Depot Archives)

* Invasion Post Office - James Brady.

Birmingham looking for a prostitute who might rent us her bed while she slept somewhere else. When we were unsuccessful we went to the American Red Cross Club and asked for a room. The night clerk laughed. And he laughed again when we asked if we could sleep on a couple of chairs or tables. In the end we went into the lounge which had G.I.s sleeping on, under and next to everything. Somehow we found enough floor space to spread out our raincoats."

Jean Bridgeman, nee Phillips, who was only six at the time, remembers the house that she visited in Rippingille Road. She recalls that number one was some sort of an office and that it had a telephone. Anybody visiting the base had to report here if there were any problems with the G.I.s on the estate. Between numbers one and three there was a wide space which jeeps and trucks used as an access drive to the field behind, where vehicles were parked.

Jean regularly used to visit the G.I.s living at number three as she lived opposite. She never went upstairs but she remembers going in the front room where there were bare wooden floorboards, a coal fire and three or four double bunk beds. At the side of the bunks was the soldier's kit. The walls were bare plaster, decorated with photos of family and sweethearts. There was also a poster of Betty Grable that the G.I.s would throw darts at and a painting of an indian on the wall. There were nails on the wall for hanging uniforms on and a dartboard on the door. The lights had no shades and there were blackout curtains at the windows. Jean would often take her pet dog with her when visiting. The G.I.s became attached to him and unofficially adopted him as he

Mess Hall No 13 (10th Replacement Depot Archives)

appeared to spend more time at number three than his own home.

After an evening spent drinking at the Trees Pub with some G.I.s Harry Austin was invited back to a billet in Romney Way to continue drinking and playing cards. On entering the house he was surprised to note that the banisters and staircase had been removed to burn on the fire. In order to reach the upper floor of the house the G.I.s had placed a ladder in the spot where the original staircase had stood.

Several people remember that due to a shortage of coal and firewood the G.I.s were forced to burn all wooden furniture and fittings including doors and beds in order to keep warm in the winter months. G.I. Albert Eisenkraft recalls:

"By October 1944 everything burnable in those houses - doors, toilet seats etc. were gone."

Albert remembers that the fireplaces were the only source of heat in the cold, damp houses. Marvin Wallman recalls that all his belongings got damp and that he even had to dry out his tobacco before he could put it in his pipe.

The Collingwood Centre, at the heart of the estate, had originally been built to serve as a community centre. The Americans used this building for a variety of purposes, the main one probably being administration. The central part of the building either side of the main entrance was made up of rooms which were suitable for lectures, administration and training. Major Free, Commanding Officer of the 4th Replacement Battalion, had his office here.

Charles Hinde, one of the original contingent of men to come to Pheasey, both

John Carpenter in the Projection room in Collingwood Centre (R. Webb)

lived and worked in this building. He remembers that he was billeted on the ground floor at the rear of the building and he worked in offices on the ground and first floor. The entire right wing was used as an officer's mess and seated about three hundred men. Although Charles was not an officer he was entitled to eat there as he was billeted in the building. Bob Webb, who used to attend the Children's Christmas Parties at the centre, remembers that the left hand side of the main building encompassed a well equipped gymnasium. The hall of the centre was used as a theatre and also to show films. At one end there was a stage and behind this were changing rooms. At the opposite end of the hall from the large doorway a narrow stairway led to a small projection room. In the wall there were three or four square apertures through which films were projected onto a screen above the stage. This room was where the children's parties were held. The chapel was also to be found in this building.

The 'Stars and Stripes' flew on the Community Building and the balcony above the main entrance was used by officers who took the salute when the men were parading. The Parade Ground, situated in Gainsborough Crescent, was known as 'Black Top', presumably because the ground was tarmacked. An air raid siren also stood on the top of the Community Centre.

There were several mess halls for the enlisted men. The official plan of the estate shows one in Gainsborough Crescent. Stella Davies remembers there being one in Hillingford Road while Harry and Phylis Baker and Sidney and Sylvia Barker remember one being on the corners of Rippingille Road, Moreland Road and Raeburn

Mess Hall No 12 (10th Replacement Depot Archives)

Road. Jean Phillips remembers the G.I.s based at the office at number one Rippingille Road walking through the gap between number one and number three to visit the mess hall there. Stella Davies and Patrick Wagstaff remember that there was a cookhouse in Chantrey Crescent. This used to back onto the edge of a steep incline where houses have been built now.

James Brady satirically describes his route to the mess hall from his billet:

"A row of buildings housing English civilians lay in juxtaposition to us at the foot of a series of gentle slopes of grazing land, while across the street was a huge open field. Up the street atop a steep hill lay a long, smooth, paved yard which served as a softball field. A series of pyramidal tents wound around the outer fringe and led to a low slung frame building at the other end of the field which served as a mess hall. The daily climb up this hill gave us excellent exercise and relieved us of any extra poundages we might have put on during the 'soft' voyage across the Atlantic." *

Fred Petrogallo remembers the mess hall as being a large brick built hall with a concrete floor. He recalls that there were long tables but no chairs or seats so that it was necessary to stand to eat. Personal mess kits were used which the men had to clean themselves afterwards. Tom Morrissey remembers that the mess hall he used seated three to four hundred G.I.s. He remembers the meals served there as being '*generally good*' although Bill Beatty remembers the food differently. He writes about the day after he arrived at the camp:

"Next morning the entire company came down with 'the G.I.s' a euphemism for diarrhoea."

Supply room 323rd Reinforcement Company and billets (10th Replacement Depot Archives)

**Invasion Post Office - James Brady.*

Mess Hall No 12 (10th Replacement Depot Archives)

As acting first sergeant for the company it was Bill's duty to get everyone assigned to rooms in the billets and organise supplies:

"So my first official duty , as a Yank in a foreign country, was to go to the Supply Room which, like the Mess, was run by the British army, and ask the handle barred, moustachioed British Major for a huge supply of toilet tissue. The problem was traced to the kitchen - seems like there was a lot of grease on the stove."

Hence another name for the camp was born, 'Greasy Pheasey'

Roy Fleming's father used to collect food waste from the officer's mess to convert to pig swill. Apparently he always maintained that he had the best fed pigs in Birmingham, thanks to the U.S. Army at Pheasey. Ron Crisp remembers that a Mr. Wilson also used to collect waste from the kitchens for his pigs.

Phil Tillar remembers that there was a Gas Mask testing station at Pheasey. Although he was billeted in Sutton Coldfield it was necessary for him to go to Pheasey to test his gas mask. Phil recalls that the procedure was to don a gas mask and then separately enter a room filled with tear gas. The men had to walk through the room and exit by a rear door. He recalls:

"Those whose gas masks leaked suffered and were issued new gas masks. Luckily for me I was not one of them."

Patrick Wagstaff remembers that some of the wooden school huts in Raeburn Road

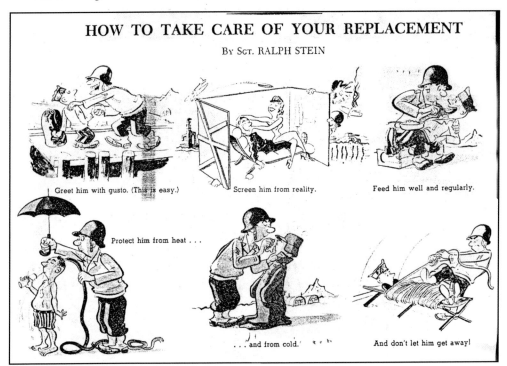

Yank Magazine

were used by the G.I.s. Harry and Phyllis Baker remember that various other buildings were erected to serve the needs of the G.I.s in the adjacent billets to this area. They remember buildings for motor vehicle maintenance, fuel bunkers and a parking area here. There was also a motor pool in Gainsborough Crescent.

Stella Davies remembers that two houses in Pomeroy Road (20 and 22) were used as a dental clinic and dispensary. There was a decontamination zone off Romney Way and a shipping area in Romney Way between Chantrey Crescent and Gainsborough Crescent from where men were 'shipped', or sent out to new assignments.

During the period prior to D.Day when the Pheasey Camp was full to capacity pyramidal and ridge tents were erected on the farmland between Queslett Road and Doe Bank Lane to take the overflow. This area became known a 'Tent City'. Ed Allard remembers being assigned to an eight man tent here. He recalls that the men were allocated two blankets each from a supply tent. As the supply sergeant was busy giving out blankets at the front of the tent Ed and his friend slipped around the back to pull more blankets loose.

Ed remembers lying in his tent at night. He recalls:

"Fog crept across the open spaces and wisped through the tent flap. In the distance we could hear dogs howling mournfully, encouraging some of us to invent ghoulish stories of the wild dogs of England who attacked at night. In the bunk below

Laugh now, but sheeping on those lumps wasn't funny!

Cartoon from 17th BPO History (J. Brady)

shivered Mendel, an unworldly lad who had been brought up in an environment of wealth and comfort and protectiveness. As he listened to the gruesome tales I reached out with a fringed scarf that I had liberated from the Red Cross Stores, letting it feed slowly through my fingers. When the fringe touched Mendel's face he screamed in a piercing falsetto, I cut loose with a loud growl and the tent erupted with departing G.I.s in long johns.

Patrick Wagstaff remembers that there was also a large marquee here filled with board games such as ludo where the men could spend recreational time. Needless to say many of the local children, including Patrick, managed to make their way there. Patrick also remembers that at the edge of the woods in Doe Bank Lane there was a rifle range. Local children used to go there to collect the spent bullets.

CHAPTER 6
No Scheduled Duties

As Pheasey Farms was a Replacement Depot its routine was different to other military camps. As Richard Minster, an officer at Pheasey states:

"Replacement Depots have no scheduled duties other than drill, calisthenics, clean up, housekeeping etc."

He continues:

"I came to this situation from a highly disciplined regular army combat division. The contrast was hard to believe. Most of them (the casual replacements) were rejects from other organisations such as Quartermaster, Engineer, Transport etc."

Richard's specific duties at Pheasey were censoring mail, issuing new clothing and equipment and interviewing casuals so as to establish pay data.

2nd Lieutenant Bill Rumold spent a year at Pheasey as Motor Pool Officer. He too came from the regular army. He had arrived in Liverpool in October 1943 in an American ship manned by the British Navy. From Liverpool he travelled to Whittington by train. On his arrival at Whittington he discovered that the Table of Organisation for the barracks had been changed so that he was no longer required there as part of its complement of officers. He spent a month there with no specific duties, then he decided to help out at the motor pool as he had been in the oil business in civilian life.

When Colonel Kilian saw that he had made himself useful in this way he interviewed him for the job of Motor Pool Officer. Shortly after this there was a disciplinary matter involving the current Motor Pool Officer at Pheasey. This officer was sent for and Bill was assigned to Pheasey to take over the position there.

The Motor Pool at Pheasey consisted of approximately 25 vehicles at this time (as opposed to nearly 200 at Whittington). The majority of the vehicles were two and a half ton 6x6 GMC trucks. There were also two or three British ambulances, three or four jeeps and a number of motor cycles. The motor cycles were mainly used by the M.P.s for convoy control. Bill recalls that he enjoyed riding the Harley Davidsons although if he had to drive over a cobblestone road, of which there were a number in the area, he preferred to drive a jeep.

Aswell as running the motor pool Bill's duties included training the replacement troops. If he had any free time he would spend it working with the troops under his command. It was also necessary for him to travel to places as far apart as Southampton or Scotland to pick up new replacement troops bound for Pheasey. While at Pheasey Bill was promoted to 1st Lieutenant. He remembers that his salary rose to $175 a month plus an allowance for quarters and a marriage allowance.

In late 1944 events on the continent during the Battle of the Bulge caused a number of hospitalised soldiers, who were not fit to be sent back into combat, to be sent to Whittington to retrain as truck drivers. The Transportation Officer at Whittington, Captain Robert E. Rosey, wasn't enthusiastic about carrying out their training so he ensured that Bill was assigned back to Whittington so that he could take over the job. From Whittington Bill was sent to Salisbury Plain to train men from non-combatant units for combat

In early 1944 the 17th B.P.O. arrived at Pheasey. This unit had been assigned to work alongside the 1st B.P.O. in Sutton Coldfield as it had been doing while billeted at Whittington Barracks. James Brady recalls:

"We were to continue work in three shifts at the 1st B.P.O., each group changing shifts every seven days. I remember that night shift in the stuffy overheated directory where it took almost superhuman effort to stay awake. (Although most of the time all it took was a tug on the shoulder by Lt.s Shiedy or Nordstrom.) And I remember the 'break' at 4:00 a.m. when we took the chance to flop on the nearest mail sack for ten or fifteen minutes or more if we succeeded in finding a spot impossible for detection.

"There were some things that helped keep us awake too. Jim Davis' raucous laughter, Joe Quirk's booming voice every once in a while as he painfully contrasted these days with the gay old ones at the New York Embarkation Post Office. The T./5s whose eyes swept searchingly over the group in eager anticipation - just waiting for someone to signal for help in deciphering an enigmatic address. We really enjoyed watching Izzy Dolansky, Les Devore, Lou Palermo and Lyman Ostrander bobbing and

Athletic Field Pheasey (10th Replacement Depot Archives)

weaving through the aisles, hopping to every puzzled one's beckon and call." *

While at Pheasey the 17th B.P.O. went through some reorganisation. At first this was not popular as James Brady recalls:

"Just as we had begun to know each other more intimately orders came down breaking us into various detachments. We were no longer companies, we were now detachments. Standing in formation waiting to be told to which detachments we were assigned we fervently hoped that many fast friendships would not be broken up. Alas many of us found to our displeasure that we were in one detachment while our buddies were in another.

"On May 8 Detachments A and B were activated. Major James J. Doherty was named Commanding Officer of Detachment A and had Lt.s John Azerdo, Albin Augustin, John Plummer and David Hymes as his assisting officers. The last named lieutenant had, on this day, been transferred from the 1st to the 17th B.P.O. Ninety nine men comprised the enlisted roster of this detachment which was attached to the First U.S. Army. Captain Charles Hare took over the reins of Detachment B with Lt.s Edward Nordstrom, Friedrick Schoenbrodt and William Shiedy as his assistants. Ninety six men were assigned to their detachment and all were attached to Advance Section Communication Zone.

"So there it was. We could still see our buddies during off duty hours but we found ourselves also making new friends and before long the entire outfit assumed the pattern of a well knit family set up. Almost everyone knew everyone else." *

Even within the Replacement Battalions there was some movement during their time at Pheasey. On 20th March 1944 the 295th Replacement Company (4th Replacement Battalion) were detailed to duty at Camp Stanley, Bridgnorth, Shropshire, as an interior guard company. The unit consisted of three officers, plus one medical officer, and 231 enlisted men. The company entrucked at Pheasey at 1300 hours and arrived at Camp Stanley at 1520 hours, having taken nearly two and a half hours to travel 35 miles. The company used Camp Stanley as a base and put out detachments to four other nearby camps for guard duty, these being Camp Davenport, Camp Coton Hall, Camp Kinlet Park and Camp Sturt Common. The tour of guard duty was relatively uneventful apart from the first two and a half days when it was necessary to repair a water main. To quote the company historian:

"This experience proved that there is considerable engineer talent in the company." +

By the end of the month advance details of the units to be stationed at the aforementioned camps arrived and took over so that the 295th could return to Pheasey which it did at 1315 hours an 29th March, arriving back at Pheasey at 1615 hours. Commanding officer, 1st Lieutenant Clifford F. Soukuf wrote at the time:

"The experiences gained during this guard duty were incredibly profitable. Not only did every member of the community learn valuable lessons in actually operating under field conditions but they also gained new knowledge about leadership,

+ *Unit History 4th Reinforcement Battalion,* * *The Invasion Post Office - James Brady.*

command , supply and cooperation." *

In April 1944 it was necessary for the 294th Replacement Company (4th Replacement Battalion) consisting of three officers and 624 enlisted men, to leave for Stafford County Technical College. The advanced party of one officer and six enlisted men departed at 1000 hours. It took four and a half hours to move the entire company in three echelons. By 2145 hours the whole company had arrived at the college.

Stafford College was a large three storey high building in the centre of the town. On the ground floor was a large mess hall, kitchen, company orderly room, supply room, storage room, billiard room and day room. There were 25 rooms of various sizes on the first and second floors where the men were billeted while there was a large gym on the fourth floor.

The company were to perform roughly the same duties while at Stafford as they did at Pheasey. The training schedule was somewhat limited because of the lack of training aids, equipment and suitable drill fields. For five mornings a week there was a road march whilst in the afternoon the company were taken to a large field a quarter of a mile from the college for baseball, softball, football (American) and soccer (English).

The enlisted men who came to Pheasey as replacement troops found that on the whole their duties were undemanding. Tom Morrissey describes a typical day at Pheasey, he admits:

"Our days at Pheasey were somewhat easy even when we were assigned to a detail, K.P., Guard duty etc."

He recalls:

"The day started at 5:30 a.m. when the troops had to fall out in formation in the building yards for reveille. We were required to respond with the word 'here' when our names were called - which in army parlance for the most part was 'Yo'. 'Yo' was a big help when one was covering for a buddy who was not in formation for whatever reason. Of course this couldn't be easily done if many men were missing from the formation. After reveille was tidy up time - washing, shaving etc., cleaning of billets and bedmaking in a military manner.

"During the afternoons, especially if casual officers were available we attended classes and studied such things as weapons and weapon stripping, even in some cases enemy weapons. We learned to strip a captured German machine gun, which was an amazingly easy thing to do."

This was the MG42 which fired 1250 rounds a minute. Later, in combat, Tom was able to attest to the rapid fire capability of this weapon. He remembers that:

"It was so fast and hard to control that the Germans used flanking, plunging fire. We learnt that if the first burst did not get you chances were it wouldn't get you and although it was very frightening many walked through its fusillade after hitting the ground on the first burst."

Tom continues:

*History of the 10th Replacement Depot.

"We also covered lectures on other German weaponry such as the V1 and V2 rockets. Aircraft identification and an array of other things military were programmed in. We also took long hikes through the northerly end of the camp."

John Carpenter recalls the time that a British N.C.O. came to the camp to train the G.I.s in the use of the bayonet. Apparently, despite the seriousness of the subject, many found the sight of the N.C.O. charging at a dummy armed with a bayoneted rifle, screaming blood curdling cries, highly amusing. The men would train on the playing fields where they would dig trenches to practice in. Rachel Barton remembers that when the children had the opportunity they would go up there to look for spent ammunition.

Albert Eisenkraft remembers attending lectures on how to behave in England. On the days when officers were not available for lectures and training Tom remembers that:

"We played softball mostly on the blacktop and also did close order drill which later came in handy for parades."

Drill layed a large part in the G.I.s time at Pheasey. Pat Capasso remembers that:

"The days were made up of interminable periods of drilling and marching through camp."

All the men were expected to take part in drill. Tom Morrissey remembers that even the G.I.s who had taken part in the D-Day landings, who were recovering from their ordeals at Pheasey, were not exempt from this duty.

Motor Section Pheasey parking lot, showing buses (10th Replacement Depot Archives)

Drill became a spectator sport and many of the residents on the estate remember watching the men marching up and down the roads outside their houses. Vic Tims remembers:

"Watching the G.I.s parade and carry out various drill routines created a certain fascination for young and old alike."

He recalls that the men often assembled on the carpark of the Trees Pub. From there squads would march up the hill along Collingwood Drive. On reaching the Collingwood Centre the troops would turn left onto the tarmac forecourt in front of the main entrance. The Commanding Officer would take the salute and then the men would continue to march past exiting out of the driveway and back onto the road before continuing to march around various roads of the estate.

Often there would be a band at the head of the parade, which would be led by a Drum Major. Bob Webb remembers the time that there was a new Drum Major who was unfamiliar with the route:

"On reaching the Community Centre instead of turning left the drum Major continued straight ahead followed by the whole contingent much to the consternation of a very irate Commanding Officer and much to the amusement of the civilian onlookers."

Patrick Wagstaff recalls one occasion when the band were transported in jeeps at the head of the procession. He remembers thinking how comical they looked.

Tim Westwood used to watch the G.I.s parading on Sundays. The parade would commence at the Old Horns Pub and continue up the Queslett Road. He comments that there always seemed to be a lot of men and they appeared to 'swing' along rather than actually march. G.I. John Carpenter contrasts the marching of the G.I.s with the British troops that he had observed:

"Boy, they were really spick and span. Their marching was immaculate, all in step and arms swinging together. When our guys stepped out we just slouched along, waving to folks on the sidewalk."

Tom Morrissey remembers that a detail was formed of about company strength which paraded through various English towns and villages for about four days or evenings a week. He remembers marching through Sutton Coldfield and Birmingham city centre amongst other places. Tom comments that he enjoyed taking part in parades, particularly when the 10th Replacement Depot Band came to lead the men.

In April 1943 Walsall held a Wings For Victory Parade. The Army Nurse Corps unit that was stationed at Pheasey at the time took part in it. In August 1943 there was another parade of American troops through Walsall. The reporter for the Walsall Observer gave this commentary on the event:

"The American Baseballers last Saturday afternoon gave Walsall a stimulating stir. The march of their band through the town won the admiration of the people who lined the streets. The band put vim into their playing and their leader saw to it that they lived right up to the reputation of their country for unfailing liveliness.

"All who saw the march felt better for the experience especially more energised and equal thereafter to extra hours on the garden or in some other essential war winning service.

An occasional stir of that kind does good especially in helping Walsall to grasp some idea of what energy and enthusiasm means."*

Tom remembers that the working day at Pheasey finished at about 1630 to 1700 hours when retreat formation was held:

"A bugler sounded 'retreat' as the Stars and Stripes were lowered and we saluted. After retreat we prepared for the evening meal and were free to do as we pleased until taps were sounded at 2300."

When asked for his memories of his time at Pheasey Tom replied:

"Who could forget their 'in limbo time' and being part of the cliche 'they also serve who stand and wait.' It was stand and wait without specific duties or programmes."

Pat Capasso confirms that he also spent time sitting around and kicking heels waiting for information of impending postings.

Earl Lovelace also remembers that while he was at Pheasey he had a lot of free time. When he arrived at Pheasey he had no specific duties so:

"I made friends with a 2nd Lieutenant and worked out a deal with him. After he went to his duties in the morning I would get to his quarters, keep the fire going, straighten up and carry out any errands that he would leave on a note. It was mostly going down to the Trees Pub. I would clean the beer bottles and take them to be refilled and sometimes pick up a bottle of gin if they had it. It worked for me as I had a nice warm place to spend my day and do whatever I wanted. I did a lot of reading."

For many of the men one of the more tiresome duties of camp life was K.P. but, much to his friends' surprise, John Carpenter volunteered for this detail. However he had ulterior motives and shortly after he took on this duty his girlfriend's family's larder became much better stocked with such scarcities as sugar. Other items such as sausages surreptitiously disappeared from the cookhouse and reappeared at John's billets. Having no oven it was necessary to cook the sausages on the open fires in the room. John recalls:

"We had one hell of a job lighting those little coal fires without kindling wood."

The problem was solved by chopping up the few items of wooden furniture and fittings in the houses.

The majority of the casuals based at Pheasey as replacement troops spent very little time there as ostensibly it was just a transit camp. 2nd Lieutenant William Brothers spent just under three weeks at Pheasey in 1944 and he considered this a longer than average period. He recalls:

"I had been in the army just long enough to learn not to volunteer for anything which probably accounts for my stay so long at Pheasey."

On 26 April he was assigned to Ordnance Section, Central Base Section on Temporary

*Walsall Observer.

Duty. He remembers that Temporary Duty, or TDY as it was known, was generally unpopular with the officers as permanent assignments were preferred.

Enlisted man, Alan Raffauf took various tests while stationed at Pheasey to decide which permanent post he would be best suited for. He passed the typing test and was sent to Quartermaster Headquarters. He reminisces:

"The tests there in camp provided me with a non-combat job which could have saved my life."

CHAPTER 7
Off Duty

As many of the G.I.s at Pheasey were unfamiliar with the area surrounding the base, much off duty time was spent in the camp whiling the time away until the next assignment. The men often spent that off duty time writing letters to friends and family back home or just sitting in their billets exchanging stories. William Brothers remembers that he and his colleagues kept themselves occupied playing poker with sixpences.

James Brady recalls:

"For the first time since we left the States athletics became an integral part of our off duty hours. Of course we were still plagued with the usual calisthenics, close order drill and gas mask drill, but in the afternoons (when we weren't working the day drill) or evenings and on Sundays, softball games would be in progress on the bumpy field behind our quarters.

"A regular softball league had been formed among the various detachments. The officers banded together and formed a single entry. We got quite a kick out of watching the games, some of which were very well played and others had the spectators rollicking in glee from the first to the final out.

"Some fellows took the games very seriously as if their lives depended upon the victory, while others looked upon them as enjoyable diversions from letter pitching and close order drill. One of the highlights of the shortlived season was the victory the officers, usually on the short end of a lop-sided score, gained over one of the detachments." *

The 294th Replacement Company (4th Replacement Battalion) also had a softball team captained by 1st Sergeant Donald Hughes. On 15th March 1944 a league was organised so that the team could compete with other unit teams in a Depot Softball League. The 294th were victorious in their first game which they won 9-7.

Another sport which often took place on the base was boxing. Earl Lovelace remembers going to the gym in the Collingwood Centre to watch the young boys box. He preferred going here to the pub as he didn't drink and also the boxing matches were free.

The Community Centre was often used to provide entertainment for the men on the base. Dances were regularly held in the auditorium. William Rumold recalls that:

"The Special Service people would arrange for girls to attend the dances by contacting local schools and offices. As the motor officer I would arrange to transport the girls to the dances and return them to their communities afterwards. The soldiers and the girls seemed to have a genuine good time. The dances helped to relieve a lot of tension and provided the chance for the young Americans to get acquainted with a

* *Invasion Post Office - James Brady.*

group of wonderful people."

Concerts were also occasionally held at the Community Centre. Ron Crisp remembers organising one featuring Charlie Chester. Charles Hinde, possibly referring to this concert recalls:

"A British entertainment group presented a fine program of music and entertainment one evening shortly after our arrival. This was very much appreciated."

On two occasions the local Home Guard, who had their headquarters at The Trees, organised concerts for the Americans at the Community Centre.

Bill Rumold remembers a concert in 1944 which featured Mickey Rooney as Master of Ceremonies. Apparently Mickey came on and gave his opening speech which was:

"Hell, I'm not standing in a hole, I'm just short."

At the end of the show he announced that the entertainment unit he was attached to would shortly be split into smaller units which would be dispersed around the country to aid the morale of the troops both in England on the continent.

Mickey Rooney had been drafted into the army in 1943 when he became part of a unit of approximately 25 entertainers who were attached to Special Service. Special Service was responsible for educating and upkeeping the morale of the men at the base they were attached to. This particular unit was billeted for a short time at Whittington Barracks.

Those that served with Mickey Rooney testify that he was a 'regular army guy'

Old Horns Pub, Queslett Road (Edward Atkinson)

who lived in army barracks and carried out K.P. duties etc. as all soldiers would be expected to. He asked that no one would unduly bother him and that he would be treated like any other soldier and not as a film star.

Mr. Rooney was often seen around the Lichfield and Walsall area. Dennis Flynn remembers that while on leave he stayed at the George Hotel, on The Bridge in Walsall. Mrs. Moore remembers seeing him and child singing star, Bobby Breen (who was probably in the same unit as Mickey) walking up the steps there. She and her friend shouted 'Hello, Mickey' and he turned and waved.

Eva Attree (nee Cox) remembers hearing that her Hollywood screen idol would be at The Blue Boar in Shenstone one evening so she and her friends cycled over there. On her arrival she remembers being disappointed at what she saw. She could not believe that the pimply youth she saw there was the movie star whom she had admired so much.

Films, perhaps some featuring Mickey Rooney, were shown in the auditorium of the Community Centre. Patrick Wagstaff, a youngster at the time, remembers that the G.I.s let him in to watch several movies there. He also remembers that he was often in trouble with his parents for staying there until the early hours. Terry Westwood, also a schoolboy at the time, recalls that one G.I. took him into the projection room to show him how everything worked.

Another meeting place for the off duty soldiers was the 'Old Barn'. This building was, as the name suggests, originally a barn for Pheasey Farm and was situated where

The Odeon Cinema, Kingstanding, which became a listed building (Kingstanding Library)

Constable Close is now located. After the war it was used as a community centre when the original community centre was put into use as a school. It was demolished in the late 1960's. The G.I.s played darts and snooker there. Dances were also held in the building.

Mabel Cooke recalls the occasion that a concert was held in one of the Mess Halls. She remembers waiting at the bus terminus with her sister, Lucy, hoping to catch a glimpse of Gracie Fields, who was to sing at the concert. Miss Fields soon arrived in a chauffeur driven Rolls Royce so the girls followed the car to Number 12 Mess Hall. On approaching the entrance they were informed that the concert was for military personnel only. However they were permitted to stand by the partially open doors of the hall from where they were able to see the temporary wooden platform that had been erected to serve as a stage.

Naturally the local pubs around Pheasey were patronised by the G.I.s. The Trees (now renamed Schofields), whose landlord was Billy King, had opened in 1938. Terry Westwood remembers that the Trees served Atkinsons beer, which many locals didn't appreciate. When the Americans arrived Mr. King decided to establish the right wing of the pub as an Officer's Club. Civilians were allowed in this room but enlisted men were not.

In the other wing Harry Austin remembers teaching a sergeant to play darts. This sergeant enjoyed the game so much that he built a wooden case with closing doors for the dartboard in the pub. Apparently this case hung in the pub for several years after the war.

Original Kingstanding Pub on Kingstanding Circle (Kingstanding Library)

Charles Hinde remembers that for a short period during 1943 the Trees was put off limits to G.I.s, presumably because there had been some trouble there. Patrick Wagstaff remembers seeing several scuffles amongst the G.I.s outside the pub. He also remembers that opposite the Trees was a fairground, which the G.I.s frequented.

The Old Horns was the other pub situated on the perimeter of the estate. Terry Westwood remembers his uncle telling him that the glasses at The Old Horns were reserved for the American patrons. He recalls his uncle asking his mother for a jam jar to take with him when he went to drink there. Harry Baker and a few of the other regulars taught the G.I.s that patronised that establishment how to play darts and dominoes.

Bob Adams remembers an occasion when, as he entered the pub, he saw about seven G.I.s seated around a table. Each G.I. had about five bottles of beer in front of him. While one of the men went to the toilet, a group of M.P.s came in and rounded the others up. On returning to the table the one G.I. was surprised to find that all of his colleagues had disappeared. Bob and his friends were not slow in coming forward to sit with him and drink the beer that was left on the table.

The G.I.s patronised other pubs in the Great Barr / Perry Barr / Kingstanding area. Those we know about are: The Deer's Leap on the Queslett Road; The Drake's Drum on the Aldridge Road; The King Charles and the Mount, both on Kings Road; The Kingstanding on Kingstanding Circle and The Crown and Cushion at Perry Barr.

Richard Minster used to frequent the Parson and Clerk on Chester Road. The landlord was Frank Jolly, who Richard remembers as *"having the temperament of a*

Deer's Leap Pub, Queslett Road (Betty Clewley)

bear with a sore paw." However Richard still enjoyed going there as the pub had a dance floor and a victrola.

Many of the men also attended the pubs further into Birmingham like: The Castle by the central fire station; Yates Wine Lodge in Corporation Street; The Midland Hotel in New Street; The Falstaff, The Camp and The Beehive, all in Bull Street. (The latter three have since been demolished.) One paratrooper, who was stationed at Pheasey for R and R remembers going to the Cattle Market Hotel where there would be a ceremonial opening of the solitary nightly bottle of Scotch. He remembers that there would be forty or more people there all clamouring for a drink.

Although the G.I.s had the opportunity to watch films in the auditorium of the Community Centre, many attended the local cinemas, the nearest being the Odeon (now a Bingo Hall) on Kingstanding Circle. This was a popular venue and James Brady remembers that:

"You had to rush down to the movie house an hour ahead of time to make sure you would get a seat." *

This cinema was particularly convenient for the men as there was a fish and chip shop opposite in Kettlehouse Lane. The chip shop was very popular with the men. James Brady remembers:-

"The queues of soldiers and civilians that stood waiting for this English version of French fries in the little store near that mammoth Odeon Theatre in Kingstanding." *

Charles Hinde standing by the 29A B'ham City Bus Outside Collingwood Centre (C. Hinde)

*Invasion Post Office – James Brady.

Mary Hood remembers seeing G.I.s, particularly M.P.s, coming out of there carrying fish and chips in their upturned helmets.

Apparently the owner of the premises had also been prevailed upon to act as a contact between dating couples who would regularly leave written messages and letters at the shop for their respective partners to collect. This method proved useful if one of the couple could not make a previously arranged date.

There was also a fish and chip shop on the perimeter of the Pheasey estate. It was situated next door to the Post Office in Beacon Road. Apparently the owner allowed G.I.s to eat their fish and chips and drink their beer in his living room.

The Americans would also attend dances in the area around the base. Every Friday and Saturday night dances were held at Kingstanding Community Centre, situated on the Kingstanding Circle. One of the local bands who regularly played there was 'Hugo Morris and his Community Orchestra.'

A number of the G.I.s from Pheasey used to travel into Birmingham to see the night life. Dennis Flynn remembers that:

To catch a bus for the city at the Circle, Kingstanding, in those days was like entering a war zone. There were Yanks everywhere. They would see the bus coming and suddenly converge on it en bloc when it came to a halt."

The Americans were instrumental in securing a bus service to run to the Pheasey estate as previous to their arrival the bus had begun and ended its route at Kingstanding Circle. The residents were grateful to the Americans for securing this

Waiting for fish and chips (17th BPO History, J. Brady)

*Invasion Post Office – James Brady.

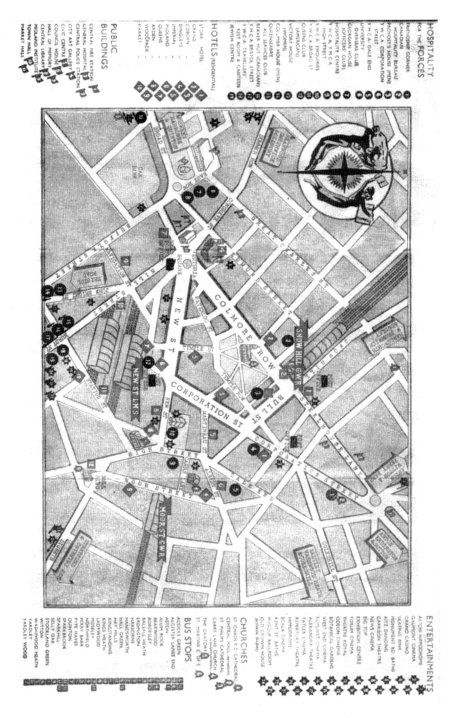

The Services guide to Birmingham and surrounding districts, given to G.I.'s at Pheasey. (K.Sell)

amenity for them. The bus running on the new route from city centre to Pheasey was designated the number 29A whereas the bus stopping at the terminal at Kingstanding Circle was 29.

G.I. James Brady was glad to have -:

" - - - *the opportunity to visit Birmingham, the second largest city in England and core of its industrial activities. To those of us who lived in or near New York City, the large double decker buses that took us to Birmingham revived nostalgic memories of the same type of vehicles that sped up and down Fifth Avenue.*

"The ride to Birmingham was also a beautiful one through vistas of multicoloured floral gardens that accentuated quiet and peaceful villages until we came to the outskirts of the city. For the first time we were gazing upon ruins of war. The dreadful effects of air bombardment were evident in sections of this large city but much of the damage had been almost completely repaired by this time."*

James remembers that Birmingham -:

" - *had quite a bit to offer in the way of entertainment*"*

He and his colleagues visited the American Red Cross Club in Stephenson Place, The Queensbury All Services Club in Hill Street and the Casino, a dance hall situated in Corporation Street.

The Casino was particularly popular with the G.I.s based in the Birmingham area as it held a dance with a 'Big Band' every Monday afternoon aswell as evening dances. This was particularly convenient for the men who regularly worked a night

Kingstanding Hotel and Odeon Cinema. (Kingstanding Library)

*Invasion Post Office – James Brady.

shift, such as the men of the 17th B.P.O. Frank Field remembers that 'liberty trucks' would pick the G.I.s up from the Casino to take them back to Pheasey after a dance.

Weekly coach tours from Pheasey were also arranged for both officers and enlisted men enabling them to visit places of historical interest such as Stratford on Avon, Lichfield, Tamworth and Warwick.

Another form of transport popular with the G.I.s was the bike. Many of the men acquired bicycles to aid them to explore the local areas. Earl Lovelace and his friend, Jack Basso clubbed together to buy one which they took turns to use.

Alf Goode, a resident on the estate, remembers cycling one Sunday on his tandem from Lozells, where his girlfriend lived, to Ebenezer Gospel Hall at Kingstanding. His journey took him through Perry Barr and past Wellhead Lane where there were a number of G.I.s standing around as they had missed the last transport back to Pheasey. One of them hailed him for a lift, so Alf let him sit on the back. At this point Alf was already tired as he had spent the day cycling around Worcester. He recalls:

"I let him do the pushing as he was a hefty bloke."

Nevertheless the couple had to dismount at Aldridge Road as they couldn't manage to cycle up the hill.

The Americans from Pheasey often attended the local churches like Beeches Baptist Church in Beeches Road, Victory Gospel Hall in Kettlehouse Lane and Carrs Lane Church in the city centre.

Towards the end of the war educational courses were offered to all American servicemen serving in Europe. Weekend lecture programmes were available at Birmingham University or full week schedules could be arranged for those who wished to attend Oxford or Cambridge. In March 1944 it was noted in the official records that:

"Staff Sergeant Norman Turcotte (of the 293rd Replacement Company) *went on D.S. at Oxford University to take a general cultural course offered to Allied Soldiers."* *

There were many more venues around Birmingham that afforded entertainment to the G.I.s from Pheasey. The Repetory Theatre (The old Rep.) in Birmingham often had playbills featuring Greer Garson, who began her career there. The Hippodrome also used to provide entertainment in the form of plays and concerts. Vera Stanley remembers going there with a G.I. to hear Vera Lynn sing in concert. The Town Hall was another venue that provided concerts and dances for civilians and servicemen and women.

* *History of the 10th Replacement Depot.*

CHAPTER 8
'Not Half so dull as Cricket'

The G.I.s from Pheasey were also evident in and around Walsall and its suburbs. Several buildings around the town had been requisitioned by the U.S. Army to use as an overflow for the Whittington and Pheasey barracks. In 1944 the 18th Field Artillery Battalion was stationed in Walsall as was the 302nd Signal Operations Battalion. Jack Haddock remembers seeing a contingent of men using St. Patrick's Church Hall in Stafford Street. He recalls watching the soldiers 'move in'.

"American army trucks were outside delivering beds and cooking utensils and by the following day some fifty or more G.I.s had made it their home for about six months. A few weeks later the recreation field near Bulls Bridge, known as Rue Meadow, became a camp for an American Motor Transport Company. Approximately 500 G.I.s were billeted in large bell tents, and their presence did not go unnoticed by the local females!

Most of the Yanks soon got invited out to tea by the ladies and on the whole got on well with the local working class people. The local children did very well with gifts of chewing gum, sweets and ice cream. Some of the lady's fathers soon began to acquire packets of Camel cigarettes and other expensive brands.

The company parked its lorries on the corporation tip in Mill Lane, alongside the Fordbrook, running parallel with Borneo Street. we lads, train spotting on Ryecroft Shed, soon investigated these strange looking trucks. At the entrance to the tip were two armed guards both chewing gum. we enquired what manufacture the trucks were and we soon became familiar with Studebakers, Dodges, Chevrolets and G.M.C.s. The Yanks on guard were quite astonished when we enquired what G.M.C. stood for. One of them replied:

'Lads, it stands for General Motors Corporation, the most powerful institution in North America and most of the world for that matter. It is in fact our God, for its wealth is supreme and we shall eventually rule this world.' "

Malcolm Evans' family lived in Borneo Street and he remembers members of the American army medical unit that were also billeted there. Malcolm, a child of eight or nine at the time, was a sickly child. Unfortunately the family doctor had told Malcolm's family that he could do nothing for Malcolm. The men of the medical unit gave Malcolm a dosage of penicillin, which was a new treatment at this time and was not widely available. To Malcolm's G.P.'s surprise the penicillin soon restored Malcolm to full health.

Jack Haddock remembers that Americans were also billeted in the church hall which was situated underneath the church in Mellish Road. Jack remembers watching the men marching from the church to the Grammar School playing fields in

Birmingham Road for training and P.T. exercises.

Walsall Airport was occasionally used by American airmen. Edward Holmes remembers seeing two P47 Thunderbolt fighter aircraft landing there. On one occasion a B17 Flying Fortress (Heavy Bomber) attempted to land there but those on duty in the Control Tower sent a flare up to warn the pilot that the runways were not long enough for such a plane so he carried on to Castle Bromwich Aerodrome.

Shortly before D-Day Edward recalls that an airman named Tex landed at the airfield in a Piper cub. His plane was allocated a small part of the airfield where its wings were painted with black and white stripes. Later Edward was to discover that the stripes were invasion markings that would serve for identification for the Allied troops on D-Day.

Walsall often provided entertainment for the G.I.s at Pheasey. Charles Hinde remembers attending musical programmes at Walsall Town Hall. Several concerts were produced there. The Town Hall was the venue for an 'All star Variety Show' produced by the 10th Replacement Depot. The reporter from the Walsall Observer was particularly impressed with the female impersonator who:

"- - - was so effectively made up that he might have deceived even the ladies in the orchestra." *

The female impersonator was Gene Cohen, who, in civilian life, had been costume designer and director of the Footlight Theatre in Holywood. Apparently he particularly amused the audience when he produced a piece of celery from his bosom. Billy Taff, who had appeared in numerous broadway hits and also in a number of films before the war played various roles in the concert. In pre war days Billy Taff had been a dancing partner to such celebrities as Betty Grable, Ruby Leder and Sonja Henie.

Shelfield Senior School also played host to concerts produced in aid of the 'Rushall Comfort Fund'. The 10th Replacement Depot Band played at some of the concerts at this venue. On New Years Day 1945 Shelfield School was the venue for a 'Hello America Ball' where both the 10th Replacement Depot Band and Carl Wynne and his ballroom orchestra played.

In July 1944 the 10th Replacement Depot Band played to a large audience on the bandstand stage in the Arboretum. The Walsall Observer relates:-

"It was certainly an acceptable 'cargo' of music and mirth that the party unloaded. Inasmuch as it included rather more swing and hot numbers than we are accustomed to and was presented at top speed, the programme could perhaps be described as having a typical American atmosphere."

In 'Salute the Soldier Week' in May 1944 there was a ball held at Walsall Town Hall where the 10th Replacement Depot performed an American Army cabaret. On the Saturday previous to this the 'Salute the Soldier Parade' took place through Walsall. All of the civil defence organisations were involved aswell as the Boy Scouts, Girl Guides, some Dutch soldiers and American troops. It was noted in the Walsall Observer that certain undertakings were taken in deference to American customs:

*Walsall Observer.

BASEBALL

FAST AND NOVEL GAME AT BLAKENALL

ENJOYED BY BIG CROWD

Birmingham Team Beaten By The Americans

On Sunday afternoon a large crowd
gathered on the Blakenall Playing
Fields to see a baseball match between
the 10th Replacement U.S. Army team
and a team from the Birmingham
League. The game was fast and interesting and the many spectators soon
became familiar with the chief features
of the game, owing to the running commentary given by Mr. J. Riley.

Those who had never before seen a
baseball game must have been puzzled
at first by the barrage of "wisecracks"
put up by the American team to put
the batsman off his stroke. The kiddies'
hearts soon warmed to the Americans,
and whenever they thought the umpire
had made a wrong decision they let
him know all about it. The ball was
knocked into the middle of the crowd
several times and one youngster was
hit in the back. He appeared to sustain
no ill effects, however, and took it all
in good part.

The Birmingham team played a good
game but they were beaten by the
10th Replacement team, the final
score being 25—1. The greater experience and skill of the Americans
soon became evident. They had to fight
hard for every run they got but
quickly managed to establish a strong
lead. Their play seemed effortless, and
they seldom failed to hold a catch. The
Birmingham team on the other hand
seemed rather nervous and several
catches were missed owing to bad
throwing. They gave the Americans
a good game, however, and the match
was thoroughly enjoyed by the
spectators.

The game was arranged by the
Mayor's War Aid Fund Entertainments
Committee, and Councillor Truman
announced that the proceeds were expected to reach about £70. He thanked
Colonel Kilian for his co-operation and
the many people who had helped to
make the afternoon a success.

Walsall Observer 29/04/44   *Walsall Observer 12/08/44*

"It is understood the American troops will carry their colours and all service personnel viewing the parade will come to attention as is the custom in the United states, and all civilians are requested to take off their hats." *

On the morning of the parade the public had the opportunity to view an:- -

" - exhibition of American equipment in the Hatherton Road Park. - - -U.S. personnel will be present to explain details and give practical demonstrations of their equipment which will include a Sherman M4 tank, 105mm howitzer with camouflage, 505 cal. machine gun (anti aircraft and anti tank), field kitchen, small arms and other mechanical equipment. The public will be able to obtain admission by purchasing as many savings stamps as they like." *

Also in this week there was an 'All American' baseball match held at Gorway Cricket Ground in aid of the Mayor's Red Cross Fund. The reporter for the Walsall Observer had a rather one-sided view of the sport as he wrote:

"Certainly, as demonstrated by the teams of the American Forces it has the attraction of novelty as was proved by the large audience at Gorway on Saturday. It is doubtful, however, whether it would be capable of arousing sustained interest and drawing regular support as do our established national games. For one thing the skill, which is essential to success is not too apparent as it is in football and cricket, and for another the spectators find it somewhat difficult to share the excitement engendered in the players." *

The reporter also commented that:

"Not the least interesting point was a study of the list of the player's home towns given in the programme. The war has brought us many strange experiences and surely not the least remarkable of them is to sit amidst the familiar surroundings of the Walsall Cricket Ground with which such 'handy' names as Dudley, Kidderminster, Old Hill, Moseley, and Stourbridge are so closely associated and watch the activities of men from Los Angeles, Baltimore, Hollywood, Santa Rosa, Spokane, Sacramento, Minneapolis, Bellfower, Hoboken, Seanton and Pittsburg." *

In August of the previous year the Mayors War Aid Committee had organised a similar game at Gorway. This was reported under the title 'Baseball Fun' and subtitled 'Quickfire Shots by Batsmen Scare Crowd.' The reporter stated that:

" - - - over 1,600 spectators enjoyed two hours of surprises and thrills and had plenty of laughs. Incidentally, at times they felt in peril of their lives but no one was hurt. - - - Ball after ball went flying out of the ground; several times they skimmed the heads of the spectators like machine gun shots and twice went crashing through the window panes of the cricket pavilion!" +

The reporter interviewed various members of the crowd after the game to ask their opinion on it. A business man replied

"I should want to take out a substantial insurance policy before I played baseball unless they paid me the salary of Babe Ruth." *

* *Walsall Observer 6/5/44.*
+ *Walsall Observer*

while a lady commented:

"I enjoyed every minute although I was nervous when the balls came whizzing over our heads. It's a quick change game - plenty of variety, not half so dull as cricket." *

In August 1944 a baseball match took place at Blakenhall between the 10th Replacement U.S. Army team and a team from the Birmingham League. Needless to say the American team won 25 -1. The reporter wrote that the American team's play;-

"- - - seemed effortless and they seldom failed to hold a catch. The Birmingham team, on the other hand, seemed rather nervous and several catches were missed owing to bad throwing." *

The game wasn't without a casualty as:

"The ball was knocked into the middle of the crowd several times, and one youngster was hit in the back. He appeared to sustain no ill effects however and took it all in good part." *

In September the Duchess of Kent visited the Gorway Cricket Ground to see a little of the baseball match played between two American teams: 'The Easterners' and 'The Americans'. The Walsall Observer related that:

"It was to Gorway where big crowds inside and outside the ground had assembled,

RUSHALL COMFORTS FUND.

THE DANCE OF THE SEASON!
NEW YEAR'S DAY, JAN. 1st, 1945.

"HELLO, AMERICA!"
BALL

In the
SHELFIELD SENIOR SCHOOL.

DANCING - 8-0 p.m. to Midnight.

TWO BANDS!

The ALL-STAR DANCE BAND of the 10th REPLACEMENT DEPOT (by kind permission of Col. James A. Kilian);

Supported by CARL WYNNE and his BALLROOM ORCHESTRA.

TICKETS (strictly limited) 5/- Each.

From Mr. K. V. Hartshorne, 3, The Square, Rushall ('phone 3590); or any Member of the Committee.

ADMISSION BY TICKET ONLY.

Walsall Observer 23/12/44

*Walsall Observer.

that the Royal party went first on their arrival by road from Birmingham. The Duchess was accompanied by the Earl of Dudley (Regional Commissioner) and Lady Dudley; the lady in waiting, Lady Herbert and Lord Herbert wearing a khaki uniform.

"As the cars entered by the lower gate play was suspended. There was a momentary silence, but cheering burst forth as the party drove slowly round the field to the front of the pavilion where the visitors were received by the Mayor. The Duchess looked very beautiful in a long black coat and dress and dainty black hat trimmed with a single ostrich plume and velvet ribbon. Her jewellry included large pearl earrings, a pearl necklace and diamond clips on either lapel of her coat." *

After offering the Duchess a welcome to the town the Mayor presented to her some of the American Officers: Colonel Kilian, Lieutenant Colonel Aldrich, Lieutenant Colonel O.Harris and Captain R.J.Norton aswell as several of the local dignitaries.

"The Duchess then took her seat by the side of the Mayor to watch the remainder of the game, details of which were explained to her by Colonel Kilian who was given a seat on the other side of her. The borough member, Sir George Shuster, opened the baseball match by pitching the first ball. Before doing so he paid a tribute to the big part men of the American forces were now playing in so many theatres of war. A thoroughly exciting game resulted in a victory by six runs to four for 'The Americans'. At the conclusion of play the members of the two American Army teams lined up smartly for inspection by Her Royal Highness who spoke a few words to individual players and officers.

She also inspected a detachment of American WACs who had marched to the ground to the accompaniment of martial music played by the drum and bugle band of the 10th Replacement Depot. Finally she was presented with a baseball as a memento of the occasion by 'Dynamite McGoldrick, the catcher for the 'Easterners' on behalf of his team and their opponents. The crowd gave her a rousing send off as she left the ground for the Council House." *

Baseball was not the only sport that the Americans played in Walsall. In June 1944 the Arboretum was host to all American boxing matches. Again proceeds from the match went to the Mayor's War Aid Fund.

Walsall Golf Club also offered hospitality to the American Forces. In June 1944 the club received a letter which read:

"To all members of the Walsall Golf Club: Greetings Gentlemen - we trust that you will remember us. We are the three American Lieutenants who took advantage of your hospitality to borrow your own clubs in order to hack your fairways to pieces and then came into your clubrooms and imbibed large quantities of your beer at your expense.

Our employer, Uncle Sam, decided that it was time for us to move on to a new location. He's a pretty good fellow, so in spite of the fact that we didn't want to leave we decided to comply with his wishes. But we took with us memories of other good fellows from what was once to us a strange land. We'll always be grateful for your

*Walsall Observer.

kindness though we cherish the thought that what we found in Walsall was real friendship.

"We'd like to say 'Thank you' for the many things you all did to make our stay in your town such a pleasant one. Back home we have an expression that just suits people like you. 'You are a bunch of regular guys.' We hope to see you again. In any event we shan't forget you." *

On the whole the respect felt by members of the U.S. Army based at the 10th Replacement Depot and the people at Walsall was mutual and at the end of 1944 the Town Council decided to take step to:

" - - - acknowledge in some way the great help which Walsall has received in various directions from Colonel James A.Kilian and the officers and men of this unit." *

*Walsall Observer.

CHAPTER 9
Anglo-American Friendship Week

In 1945 the council decided upon a way to acknowledge both the part the American servicemen were playing in the war and also the part they were playing in the life of the town of Walsall. This acknowledgement was in the form of an Anglo-American Friendship Week. As Walsall solicitor, Mr. Addison stated, the purpose of the week was:

" - -to further understanding between our two countries, partly with the view to the prosecution of the war to a victorious end and, equally important, to ensure the continuance of such an understanding as would lead to whole hearted cooperation between the two nations in maintaining the peace of the world." *

Walsall was the first town in Britain to organise such an event. The Walsall Observer called it:

" - - -the most important event of its kind to be held in this country. - - - Other towns have recognised the help received from American forces by organising celebrations in their honour, but these have been confined to one day only. Nowhere else has there been undertaken such an ambitious effort in the promotion of Anglo-American friendship. - - - Walsall may therefore take pride in having given a lead to the country. It seems no exaggeration to suggest that if all our big towns and centres, at any rate those in which America servicemen have been stationed, followed suit it would do more than is likely to be achieved by the ordinary bonds of propaganda. It is the personal contacts that count most." *

The Mayor told the citizens that:

"I want this to be a real town effort such as we have never had before - - - but if that is to be the case we must have the cooperation of all organisations in the town. It must be a real town movement representing all sections of the community showing our faith in the future relations between the two countries. - - -We want to show as a town how much we appreciate all the Americans have done and how much they have meant to us in the war and every other way." *

There was a programme for the week's events which had forewords written by both Councillor John Whiston, the mayor of Walsall and Colonel Kilian, former Commanding Officer of the 10th Replacement Depot. Colonel Kilian wrote:

"The events of this week will be a lasting impression to me and to the American soldiers under my command, of the firm spirit of friendship, understanding and cooperation held out to all members of the U.S. Army by our neighbours, the people of Walsall.

"The tremendous mutual spirit of neighbourly comradeship demonstrated in the daily associations between Walsall residents and ourselves will serve as a guiding

*Walsall Observer.

72

beacon light to both nations as a splendid example to the world itself in how tightly cemented the bonds of unity have become between England and the U.S..

"This is the kind of understanding which, if fostered among the other people of the world, will bring peace and harmony to the troubled waters now flooding over the Dam of war. And know that with fine flowering as this Anglo-American Friendship Week continues to rise from the soil of our nations, that day of lasting peace is almost upon us."

Regrettably Kilian was fated to miss the events of the Anglo-American Friendship Week in Walsall as shortly after he wrote this foreword in January 1945 he was sent back to the States and Colonel Sleeper took over as Commanding Officer of the 10th Replacement Depot.

The U.S. Ambassador sent his greetings to the people of Walsall ending his message with:

"We knew from the letters to and from our troops who have gone to France and from their many requests to spend their leave in Great Britain that the 'American Invasion' of 1942-1944 has left behind it a warmth of sentiment unknown to allies in the past. You are giving an outward sign of that sentiment today. Let us preserve the inward reality forever in our hearts."

The activities for the week were planned to cater for a wide range of interest. The

Colonel Sleeper and Mayor of Walsall cutting cake. (Walsall Local History Centre)

* *Walsall Observer.*

majority of the events were to be free of charge to the public although during the course of the meetings a collection was to be taken for the Red Cross. During the week small pin badges were to be sold also in aid of the Red Cross. The badges displayed the emblem of the week which was the crossed flags of Great Britain and the United States.

On Monday evening, as an introduction to the week's events, there was a public meeting addressed by Professor Newell who was the head of the Institute of British American Relations. As an American himself he had a particular interest in the week. He told his audience that:

" - - *this week of friendship and hospitality is one of the finest things any town in this country has done since the invasion of Britain - the only invasion that Britain has had to suffer since the war began."* *

He went on to emphasise the importance of unity between the two nations for final victory in the war and the construction of a new world of peace, prosperity and security. He was satisfied that: - -

" - - - *all the work which had been done by his own committee and its officials and by the officers of the 10th Replacement Depot would be well worth while and that the friendship shown by Walsall people towards their guests during the week would enable members of the American forces to return to their own homes with the happiest recollections of Walsall."* *

At the beginning and end of Professor Newell's address the combined military

G.I.'s take a tour of Walsall leather goods factory (Walsall Local History Centre)

*Walsall Observer.

bands of the 1st Battalion South Staffs. Regiment and the 10th Replacement Depot played for the audience.

Professor Newell also gave a lecture to school children earlier in the day on 'American History and Anglo-American Relations'. The children were invited to compete in an essay competition using the title:'Anglo-American Relations'. A prize was presented to the winner by a member of the American forces at the end of the week.

Those interested in sport were catered for during the week. On Thursday there was an Anglo-American Aquatic Gala with an American Diving Display and a display by Walsall school children. On Friday there was an exhibition of basketball followed by a match between a team from Dolobran Athletic Club from Moseley (National Champions in 1942) and a team from the 10th Replacement Depot.

On Wednesday there were two miniature range shooting matches between teams from the 10th Replacement Depot and the 3rd Cadet Battalion of the South Staffs Regt. In one match American officers took on the Army Cadet Officers, the G.I.s won by 613 points to 587. In the other match American other ranks took on the cadets, again the G.I.s won, this time by 543 points to 523.

In the course of the week two dances were held. The first, which took place on the Thursday at the Town Hall, featured the American Stars of Swing Band and the Dance Orchestra of the 1st Battalion, South Staffs Regt. At this dance there was a jitterbug contest where the prize was six guineas. The second, held at the George Hotel on

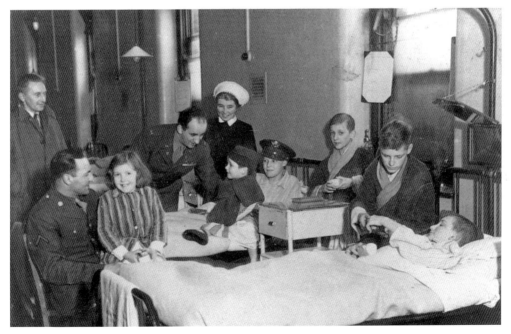

G.I.'s visit childrens ward at Walsall Manor Hospital (Walsall Local History Centre)

Friday, featured a dance band from the 10th Replacement Depot. There was a charge for tickets for the dances, the proceeds of which went to the Red Cross Fund. Tickets for the dance at The George Hotel cost ten shillings while tickets for Thursday's dance cost five shillings for civilians and one shilling and sixpence for servicemen and women.

There were also a number of concerts and shows during the week. On Wednesday there was an Anglo-American Variety Show called 'Allied Discoveries'. On Thursday members of Walsall Civil Defence and a number of American artists produced a Variety Show in Bloxwich. On Friday there was a performance of 'Let's Be Buddies' produced by the 10th Replacement Depot. There was also a Burlesque performance of Aladdin performed by the members of the Amateur Dramatic and Entertainment Society of Helliwells Ltd. with U.S. entertainers in the cast.

During the week the people of Walsall could visit an exhibition set up by the 10th Replacement depot in the Lily Hall of the Town Hall. This exhibition contained:

" - - - *exhibits relating to almost every aspect of the life of the U.S. soldier including various types of guns and rifles, gas masks, chemical bombs and special signalling telegraphic apparatus, including a medical exhibit giving a realistic illustration of how a wounded soldier would receive a blood transfusion on the battlefield.*" *

The car park in Lichfield Street held an exhibition of various types of military vehicles used by the U.S. Army.

American Stars of Swing dance band at Walsall Town Hall (Walsall Local History Centre)

* *Walsall Observer.*

During the preparation for the week the Mayor stated that he would be:

" - - - *especially pleased if shopkeepers and others in the town would make a special effort to emphasise the value of 'Friendship Week' by flying as many flags as they can throughout the period."**

Several shops displayed Anglo-American exhibits in their windows and were decorated with flags streamers and bunting, as were the public buildings in Walsall. At The Bridge, in the centre of Walsall, there was a large sign offering a welcome to American friends and allies.

The Hospitality Committee arranged for a number of American soldiers to be received as guests in Walsall homes for one or two days:

" - - - *to give them an opportunity of seeing at first hand what English home life is like."**

The Boy Scouts, Girl Guides and Girl Training Corps offered entertainment and hospitality to the troops during their weekly meetings.

Members of the Medical units based at Whittington and Pheasey visited both Manor Hospital and Walsall General Hospital during the week where they distributed candy and gum to the children who were patients there.

In the middle of the week Walsall solicitors entertained American members of the legal profession at the Council House where they discussed the differences and similarities in the laws of the two countries. At the end of the evening the Americans were invited to attend a sitting of the Walsall Magistrates Court. They were issued with

Banner presented to 10th Replacement Depot by the Borough of Walsall (Walsall Local History Centre)

* Walsall Observer.

77

a summons that read:

"That you on 7th March 1945, whilst a member of the armed forces of the United States of America, were attending a convivial evening organised by the members of the legal profession practising in Walsall at a time when it was your duty to be present in camp in order to assist in the restoration of world peace contrary to the provisions of the Lend Lease Act. You are therefore summoned to appear before the Walsall Court on Saturday the 25th of December 1955."*

On Saturday the week culminated in a parade of American and British troops accompanied by Military bands which commenced at 3p.m. The route led along Arboretum Road, then Broadway North, up Littleton Street to Stafford Street then to Park Street, The Bridge, Lower Bridge Street to the Council House in Lichfield Street where the Mayor took the salute at 4p.m.. The Walsall Observer reported that:

" At an impressive parade of over a thousand American troops on the central green at the Arboretum on Saturday afternoon the Mayor - - - presented to the 10th Replacement Depot a splendid regimental standard, from the citizens of Walsall, to mark the magnificent spirit of mutual friendship, cooperation and understanding which has always existed between ourselves and the men of the United States Army. The standard is symbolic of the comradeship and unity that were fostered during the town's Anglo-American week, for it represents the shield and eagle of the 10th Replacement Depot, surmounted by the borough coat of arms embroidered on a navy blue silk background edged with gold. On it are inscribed the words - Presented to the

G.I.'s inspecting leather goods at local factory (Walsall Local History Centre)

*Walsall Observer.

U.S. Army 10th Replacement Depot by the citizens of the County Borough of Walsall, England."*

The Mayor, presenting the banner, spoke on behalf of the people of Walsall:

"Today is a very proud day for me and for Walsall, and I am honoured, as mayor of this important town, to become officially associated with the officers and men of the U.S. Forces in the Depot. Since your soldiers began to arrive here, under the able command of that distinguished soldier, Colonel James A.Kilian, we in Walsall have tried to make them feel, if not at home, at least among friends. Many thousands of them have come here and during their stay with us their conduct and demeanour have made a great impression on us. While the officers and men have so acted they have thus become ambassadors in this country. I cannot forget that many thousands of them who were here for a short time left us to fight side by side with our own boys in the hot sands of Africa and in the mud of Italy, Holland and Belgium. Many of these soldiers with our own men have laid down their lives in the common cause and in this beautiful park today at this ceremony we especially remember their sacrifice."

The banner was accepted by the American colour party. Colonel Sleeper replied on behalf of the American soldiers:

"It is indeed an honour for me to accept on behalf of the officers and men of my command this beautiful standard. - - - We shall cherish it always as a symbol reminding us of the many happy occasions and the generous hospitality we have received from the people of Walsall. I extend to the people of Walsall on behalf of our

Presenting the Banner to the 10th Replacement Depot at Walsall Arboretum
(Walsall Local History Centre)

*Walsall Observer.

79

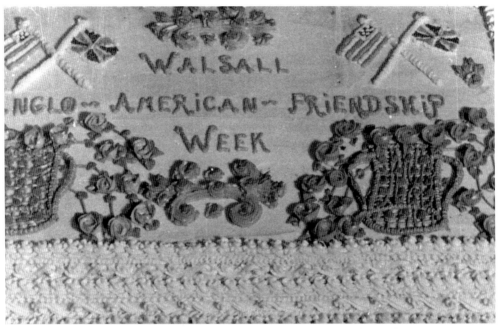

Cake to celebrate Anglo-American Friendship week (Walsall Local History Centre)

Anglo American Friendship week banner,
Insert: Pin badge sold during the Friendship week
in aid of the Red Cross (Walsall Local History Centre)

soldiers, our deep appreciation for all those acts of kindness that we have enjoyed in your town." *

A recording of the ceremony was made by the B.B.C. and relayed to the United States on the following Monday where it was broadcast by six independent stations. A number of speeches made at other events in the week were also recorded for broadcast. Some of the week's events were filmed for incorporation in a newsreel release while news concerning the progress of the week was conveyed to listeners in the United States over the American Forces Network.

At the end of the week one of the American Offices stated that:

"The one thing we are emphasising is that this movement to bring our two nations closer together is not just confined to this one week. We regard it as something to be continued as long as we are here and even after we return home." *

Colonel Sleeper commented that:

"Walsall has been extremely generous in its hospitality and very tolerant in its attitude to the American Soldier. Here in Walsall the representatives of two great nations, different in many aspects, but possessing the same ideals have made friends and I believe will continue to be friends and pursue those ideals with a singleness of purpose." *

CHAPTER 10
Birmingham Hospitality

Colonel Kilian, Commanding Officer of the 10th Replacement Depot until early 1945, was very keen to foster good community relations between his men and the people of the local towns and so was well liked by the inhabitants of both Walsall and Birmingham. In February 1945 the Walsall Observer stated:

*"Not every town, of course, has been so fortunate in the type and character of American Commander sent to it as Walsall has been. From the early days of his residence among us it has obviously been the aim of Colonel J.A.Kilian to establish and maintain cordial relations between his men and the local inhabitants."**

The people of Walsall had intended to present Kilian with an ornate silver bowl which they had inscribed: *"Presented to Colonel James A. Kilian, Commanding Officer 10th Replacement Depot, U.S. Army, As a token of goodwill and esteem and in appreciation of his ever ready helpfulness and cooperation in the social work of the town from the inhabitants of the County Borough of Walsall, Staffordshire, England 1945."*

The presentation was planned for the conclusion of the Anglo-American Friendship Week in March 1945, but to the people of Walsall's surprise Kilian was recalled to Amercia a few weeks before this event. Colonel Sleeper took Kilian's place as Commander of the 10th Replacement Depot. The Council intended to send the bowl directly to Kilian but inquiries regarding his whereabouts were unproductive and the military authorities were distinctly uncooperative when approached. Consequently the silver bowl remained in Walsall.

Later the people of Walsall and Birmingham were surprised to find that Kilian had been recalled to America to stand before a court martial for his treatment of prisoners at the stockade at Whittington Barracks. He was found guilty of aiding, authorising and abetting nine enlisted guards and three subordinate officers' cruelty to prisoners. The court found him not guilty of knowingly condoning brutality but guilty of permitting it. He was fined five hundred dollars and issued a reprimand.

While Commander of the 10th Replacement Depot, Kilian had strongly supported the Birmingham Hospitality Committee which was run in conjunction with the Lord Mayor's War Relief Fund. This organisation was active from late 1943. In July of 1944 nearly three thousand men were entertained in local homes through officially fostered contacts.

The service was entirely voluntary on behalf of the hosts and hostesses. The families who entertained G.I.s received no financial remuneration although each soldier was issued with coupons by the Hospitality Committee so that the hosts were able to supplement their usual rations. The Committee also attempted to interest the

Walsall Observer.

G.I.s in the surrounding area by arranging shows, speakers, historical tours and factory visits.

Amongst the people who registered their willingness to support the scheme were Mr. and Mrs. Arthur Lucas who lived on the Queslett Road. By the time they joined the scheme Arthur was already friendly with a number of servicemen from Pheasey. The committee chose Corporal William Stiles to spend Christmas 1943 with the couple and their eighteen year old daughter, Doreen. The Lucas family picked William up from the Y.W.C.A. on Broad Street in Birmingham at 10:30 a.m. on Friday December 24th and he stayed over the weekend.

After this occasion the Lucas's had the opportunity to show hospitality to twelve more American and two Canadians. Some stayed one or two nights with the Lucas's, others just dropped in for coffee, sandwiches or to share a meal. Doreen recalls that most of the men were homesick and that the hospitality her parents showed went some way to alleviate the problem. She remembers that the men were always eager to talk about and show pictures of their families. The Lucas family often organised informal parties for their guests. On these occasions 'singalongs' around the piano were a regular feature as Doreen was an accomplished pianist. Other evenings would be spent chatting, listening to the radio and writing letters.

One G.I., Ken Kilburn, became a firm family friend and often stayed with the family, so much so that Mrs. Lucas decided to keep a bed permanently made up for him. Ken's duties involved travelling between Pheasey and Whittington. He would often persuade his truck driver to stop the truck outside the Lucas's so that he could visit them and also, when possible, bring food and cigarettes from the camp for the family.

Unfortunately, when the officers discovered that a number of G.I.s were visiting civilian homes during their working hours there was a ruling made to prevent it. Shortly after this rule came into being Ken needed to travel from Whittington to Pheasey so he took with him his usual kit bag full of goodies for the Lucas's. In view of the new orders Ken's driver was reluctant to stop outside the Lucas's so Ken had to wait until the truck reached the perimeter of the camp opposite the Deer's Leap Pub to alight and then walk back. At this time Queslett Road consisted of a single track with hedgerows along most of its length. Anxious not to be caught by the M.P.s every time Ken saw a military vehicle approach he tossed the bag into the hedgerow and walked on without it, returning to retrieve it after the vehicle had passed. This procedure considerably lengthened Ken's walk back to the house!

Most of the men who were introduced to the Lucas's through the Hospitality Committee kept in touch and several visited when they were able. A number sent presents to show their appreciation. One G.I., Sergeant Pearlberg, had a parcel of nuts and sweets sent to the Lucas's from a New York store, an unexpected luxury in times of strict food rationing. A Canadian, Private Len Freland, asked his wife to send maple leaf broaches for Doreen and her mother.

At the end of the war the chairman of the Birmingham Hospitality Committee asked the Lucas's to make a list of the servicemen that they had been able to help. With the list Mrs. Lucas enclosed a letter which read:

"But for an occasional dance and picture show, being a country district our enjoyment has been simply home life and music. My husband has contributed financially and otherwise, my daughter has helped entertain, being a good pianist. It has meant much additional work for myself as I have carried on singlehanded with laundry and cooking, but we have thoroughly enjoyed doing it and have been happy to have made a real home for so many, our one regret being that it could not have been more owing to difficult wartime catering. I might add that everyone of these boys have been simply grand and no one could be more sorry than we to see the last of them."

Another couple who volunteered to the Hospitality Committee to be hosts were Arthur and Betty Embrey. Arthur had been seriously wounded at Dunkirk and therefore had been discharged from the army on medical grounds, it was he who suggested to Betty that they should join the scheme.

Arthur and Betty and their two sons, Trevor and Clive, opened their house in Kings Road to the G.I.s as a place for them to relax in. Clive remembers that the G.I.s used to visit his house to write letters, listen to the radio or simply to chat. The Embrey's house was warmer than the men's billets at Pheasey, particularly in the winter time.

To show their appreciation several of the Americans would bring tinned meat and fruit from the camp. One of the G.I.s, Joe Capallo, an American of Italian descent, would insist on cooking the food he brought with him. Clive remembers his spaghetti bolognaise topped with tomato ketchup which he recalls:

" - - - ran down the side like lava from a volcano."

Aswell as Joe Capallo Clive remembers Lonnie Harrel and Charles Hetrick as being regular visitors to the house. He also remembers that he and his brother were never short of gum or candy during the war.

The three men kept in touch with the Embreys after the war and in 1978 Betty and her grandson travelled to Fort Lauderdale to visit Lonnie Harrel. In a press cutting from the Fort Lauderdale News Lonnie relates how he enjoyed Betty's speciality, fish and chips. After the war the G.I.s had invited Betty to return to America with them to open a fish and chip shop, but naturally she was reluctant to leave her family.

A large number of Americans enjoyed the British 'dish' of fish and chips and they would often ask the housewives on the Pheasey Estate to cook chips for them. Bob Webb remembers the occasion that his mother cooked fish and chips for a group of G.I.s. He recalls the men's reaction when he delivered the chips to them:

"Suffice to say they were delighted with this spontaneous show of concern for their welfare and wanted to know who the chips came from, who I was and where did I live etc. A measure of their appreciation manifested itself a few days later when there was a knock at the front door. My mother was confronted by the same two soldiers to whom I had taken the chips. She was surprised to receive a large cardboard box. 'Just a few

candies for Bobby', they explained."

Because of food rationing and the shortage of cooking fat the Americans would provide a large tub of lard so that chips could be cooked for them. Edna Baker remembers that when she cooked chips in her small kitchen and served them out of the back window of her house there would be a queue of G.I.s stretching right down the path of her back garden.

Mrs. Wynn, who lived on the Beeches Estate, remembers seeing an article in the Evening Mail, probably written by the Birmingham Hospitality Committee, asking householders to be host to an American Soldier for Christmas. She decided to reply to the article as she felt sorry for the Americans who would be far away from their own homes at Christmas.

Ralph Harker, who came from Queens, New York, was the G.I. chosen to spend Christmas with the Wynns. On New Years Eve Mrs. Wynn persuaded darkhaired Ralph to do the first footing and let the New Year in. Ralph was unfamiliar with the custom and at first thought Mrs. Wynn was playing a joke on him.

Ralph got on well with the Wynns and their neighbours and carried on visiting them after Christmas. He would often bring sweets for the neighbourhood children. Ralph also brought friends with him who enjoyed the homely atmosphere, especially sitting around the Wynn's open fire.

The Wynns would often provide meals for Ralph and his friends. Mrs. Wynn remembers the occasion that she was lucky enough to have a tomato for tea. She planned to divide it into four so that everyone could have a piece, but before she could stop him Ralph, not realising the scarcity of tomatoes, ate it whole. Later, Ralph's mother sent a cake to the Wynns to thank them for their hospitality to her son but unfortunately it was stale by the time it reached them.

Ralph met several of the Wynn's relations. Mrs. Wynn's sister used to visit every weekend, often bringing a friend with her. This friend fell in love with Ralph and eventually they were married.

Many of the local residents invited G.I.s back to their homes. The majority of these families were not part of the Hospitality Committee scheme, they were just people who wanted to show friendship to the young soldiers. Iris Sidaway, living in Kingstanding, recalls that:

" - - - most of the boys seemed to prefer to be taken into English homes to be treated like one of the family, to belong, as this is what they missed the most."

Christmas was a time when the G.I.s particularly appreciated hospitality in people's homes. Ena Murcott (nee Bell) remembers the two G.I.s that her father brought back with him from the Golden Hind Pub on Christmas Day. The men enjoyed their Christmas dinner with the family although Ena noticed how nervous one of them was at the thought of going into combat in the near future.

Mrs. Procter's father often brought soldiers home from the Deer's Leap. She remembers that the Americans liked to pass around photos of their families and pets.

They enjoyed playing with the British children who reminded them of their own. Sylvia Moore remembers that when her eldest sister, Ruth, had a baby the G.I.s who visited their family enjoyed going shopping with them, pushing baby John in his pram.

Pamela Oates (nee Morrisson) met 1st Lieutenant Spiro Agnew (later to become Vice President of the United States), Shelby Foote (well known novelist) and Lieutenant Richard Minster at a dance at the Parson and Clerk Hotel on the Chester Road. The three became friends and Pamela often invited them to her home. In the week she served as an assistant welfare officer at T.R.E. Defford, an R.A.F. airfield near Pershore, so her contact with the G.I.s was limited to evenings and weekends.

Pamela's mother felt sorry for the Americans who were often lonely and enjoyed entertaining them at her home. When Richard Minster left Pheasey for Tidworth Barracks Pamela presented him with a perspex model of a mosquito plane (which he has to this day). Pamela's friendship with the two officers continued after the war through the medium of letters.

Another friendship that continued after the war was the one between American Motor Pool Officer, Bill Rumold, and the Chief Police Constable of Staffordshire County. Bill writes:

"One of my memorable contacts was with the Chief Constable of Staffordshire County, Col. Herbert P. Hunter. Colonel Hunter was a guest of Colonel Kilian for an evening of entertainment as were a number of local V.I.P.s and friends. Perchance I was assigned as an escort officer to accompany the Hunters for the evening. From that

RAINBOW CORNER CLUB
AMERICAN RED CROSS *Overseas Photo Service*

Spiro T Agnew outside his quarters (R Minster)   *Alan Raffauf (A Raffauf)*

chance meeting I had the honour of visiting Colonel Hunter, his wife, Nell, and daughter, Pauline, many times during the war years and several times after that."

When the Hunters first invited Bill to visit them he responded that it would be necessary to ask permission from Major Free, his Commanding Officer at Pheasey. Major Free not only granted permission but assigned Bill a driver to take him to the Hunter's home, Pyebirch Manor, near Eccleshall in Staffordshire. Sadly the Hunters had lost a son in a motor cycle accident the year previously so Bill found that he filled a void for the family. He regarded the Hunters as his second family. Bill writes about Britain:

"I have many great memories of your great country. My transport duties took me all over England, Wales and some of Scotland. sometimes by truck, sometimes as a troop train commander. Wherever I went I always appreciated the great resoluteness and fortitude of the British people."

Many of the housewives on the Estate took on a maternal role towards the G.I.s although some weren't much older than the men themselves. Twenty eight year old Sylvia Barker remembers a young G.I. calling out to her through the garden fence:

"Gee, ma'am, you do so remind me of my mom."

Although food rationing meant that there was hardly enough food to go round the family the locals managed to find enough to offer to their G.I. guests. Mr. and Mrs. Evetts, who lived in Hillingford Avenue, became friendly with a number of G.I.s. Two in particular Clyde, who was a cook, and Alan Raffauf, who was a clerk, visited the

Parson and Clerk Hotel, Chester Road c.1921 (Sutton Library)

Evetts regularly. Alan remembers that they always put on a good spread although he suspects that to do this they may have gone short themselves. Alan was stationed at Pheasey for just three weeks, but in that short time he says that the Evetts:--

" - - - *showed me so much warmness that it lasted these plus fifty years. It was my first meeting with a very friendly people.*"

Vera Stanley remembers that the G.I.s who came to her house could never understand why the family didn't have any coffee, but that they always enjoyed her home made apple pie. Olive White recalls that:

"*Our house was always open to them and we introduced them to tea drinking.*"

Terry, Olive's son recalls:

"*I can remember my mother telling me about some of the characters we had in our house. We had a full blooded native American (Sioux). We also had a former Pinkerton Agent and a G.I. called Jesse James who claimed to be a direct descendant. We had visits from Southerners who were still at war with the North, farm boys and New Yorkers, most of them were very young. There was a G.I. named Melvin Weiss who was a war photographer from New York. He became my sister, Lyndsey's godfather. After*

Birmingham Hospitality Committee

A SUB-COMMITTEE OF

THE LORD MAYOR OF BIRMINGHAM'S WAR RELIEF FUND

Please Reply to
Chairman's Private Address—
92 NEWHALL ST., BIRMINGHAM 3
Telephones CEN 5370, 7122

Chairman of the General Council:
THE LORD MAYOR OF BIRMINGHAM

2 - 4 EDMUND ST.
BIRMINGHAM 3
Telephone CENtral 3643-4 Telegrams Welcome, B'ham.

Officers—Executive Committee
Lord Mayor's Fund
Chairman—H. F. HARVEY
Chairman Finance Committee —F. WAIN
J. R. JOHNSON (City Treas.)
Hon. Treasurer
N. H. LEAKER (Lord Mayor's Sec.)
Hon. Secretary

Officers—Hospitality Committee
Chairman—E. T. PHEILS, D.O.
Vice-Chairman—W. H. JAMES
Hon. Treasurer | Hon. Secretary
L. B. DAVIS | H. W. GREEN
REG. BOARDMAN
Chairman—' ENTERTAINMENT '

11th October, 1945.

Dear Mrs. Lucas,

You are indeed a wonderful Hostess and the thanks of the Birmingham Hospitality Committee is tended to you very sincerely.

We are so glad you had such a happy experience with your boys. Your letter is very interesting and also the list of men you have entertained and in due course a compilation of all the present responses will be made.

Again thanking you and with every good wish.

Yours sincerely,

E.T. PHEILS. Chairman.

Mrs. Lucas,
'Rhossili' Queslett Rd,
Streetly Sutton Coldfield, STAFFS.

Birmingham Hospitality Committee 'Thank you for entertaining soldiers'

the war my family received an invitation to his wedding."

G.I., Earl Lovelace became a particularly close friend to the family. Earl was only eighteen when he arrived at Pheasey. Terry recalls:

"One night my mother asked his friend why he looked so sad, she was told that he had received a message that his mother had been killed in a car crash. Earl said that he had some compasssionate leave to come so my parents asked him to spend it at our house."

Earl, himself, recalls the White's hospitality:

"Several of us would visit them and take what food we could and anything else we could. We would spend a lot of time there, talk, play cards etc. Roland (Olive's husband) was not too healthy and one night about midnight it happened to be quite light out. Olive mentioned that she would like to make a garden in the back yard but couldn't dig the dirt, so a couple of us went out at midnight and spaded up the back yard. (At the time I thought they had a large yard but when I visited later in 1990 I was shocked to see how small it was.)

Earl and his wife visited the Whites a number of times after the war while several

THE BIRMINGHAM HOSPITALITY COMMITTEE

PRESIDENT —— THE LORD MAYOR
2-4 EDMUND STREET, BIRMINGHAM 3

To Mrs. *Embrey*

The Lord Mayor, the Members of the Lord Mayor's War Relief Fund and the Birmingham Hospitality Committee desire to offer you their very sincere thanks for so kindly entertaining, from time to time, men of the Home, Dominion and Allied Forces.

The opportunities thus afforded these men of becoming members of a family circle during their brief periods of leave are, we know, tremendously appreciated and go far towards cementing the bonds of friendship and understanding between all the Allied peoples.

LORD MAYOR, PRESIDENT

CHAIRMAN, LORD MAYOR'S WAR RELIEF FUND

MAY, 1945

CHAIRMAN, HOSPITALITY COMMITTEE

Birmingham Hospitality Committee 'Thank you for entertaining soldiers'

members of the White family visited Earl in California. As Terry states:

"we remain friends to this day. He considers us his English family."

Several local people remember that the G.I.s they were friendly with were aware of the rationing situation and would often bring them tinned fruit or meat when they came to visit. Mrs. Procter remembers that when the Americans received a food parcel from home they were mindful of the British rationing situation and would always share the parcel with the British families who had given hospitality to them.

Gwen Shelton remembers that her grandmother, Mrs. Fullylove, often put on parties for the G.I.s. Johnny Shumsky from Michigan and Eddy Grant from New York, were regular visitors to the house. Gwen recalls that the food at the parties was so good that she suspects that it was probably supplied by Johnny and Eddy. (After the war when food was still rationed in Britain, the two men sent hampers to Mrs. Fullylove which included tinned chicken and crystallised fruit.)

One evening some of the G.I.s who visited the Whites asked Olive if they could have a small party at the house. She agreed but warned them that because of the rationing situation she wouldn't be able to supply food. One of the G.I.s worked in the cookhouse so on the night of the party he arrived at the house with some butter under his cap and sausages strung around his waist. Olive only needed to supply the bread and tea.

Many locals remember the Americans with fondness for their kindness and generosity. Doreen Garner remembers that after an air raid some G.I.s would go around the shelters in people's back gardens to check that everyone was alright.

Harry Austin recalls the generosity of one sergeant that regularly gave him packs of Camel or Lucky Strike cigarettes and on one occasion gave him a pipe and tobacco.

Shelby Foote on left (R. Minster)

In Harry's opinion they also made very good drinking partners.

During the war, on Remembrance Day, Mrs.Procter used to help her father sell poppies for the British Legion. She remembers the occasion when she and her friend took a large tray of poppies and collection tins to the entrance of the camp by The Trees. They asked the guards if they could take them in the camp. She recalls:

"It was great. They made us welcome. Our tin was that heavy we could hardly carry it. They piled us high with candy and gifts."

In 1945 a group of Christians who used the Old Barn for a Sunday School decided to save up for a church building. The congregation kept a box to put coins in each week. It was an American soldier who put the first pound in the box because he wanted to support their project. A pound was a considerable sum in those days. The building that the congregation finally built was Pheasey Evangelical Church in Romney Way.

A small number of people living on and around the Pheasey Estate were not so welcoming to the servicemen based there. Derek Flynn remembers that some British people found the Americans brash and arrogant. He felt:

"The majority of the G.I.s were blessed with the gift of the gab and were capable of telling the tallest of tall stories to influence the young ladies. It was amazing to hear them tell of their fathers who owned a ranch and large spread of cattle in Colorado or expound on their daddies who were oil barons with massive oil wells in Texas, and the most amazing thing about it was the girls were prepared to believe it despite the obvious New York Bronx accent."

1st Lt Richard Minster (R. Minster)   *Ralph Harker (Mrs Wynn)*

Bob Adams had cause to get annoyed with a couple of G.I.s who often parked their jeep outside his house, in Raeburn Road, while visiting his neighbours, the Beardshaws. Finally when Bob arrived home to find the jeep yet again parked outside his house he decided to let the handbrake off so that it rolled down the road as far as the school.

There was also some resentment from the families of men in the British Forces living on the estate. As Derek Flynn states the issue of pay was: - - -

" - - - *a cause of unjustified resentment - - - I think it wasn't a question of G.I.s being paid too much but the British army paying too little!"*

Iris Sidaway writes in a similar vein:

"Overpaid the critics said, alright they were paid more than our boys but that was all credit to their government. Would our boys have refused had our government paid them more than the insulting pittance they got."

In the majority of cases the G.I.s stationed at Pheasey were made to feel welcome, not only by residents on the estate but also by those living in the surrounding area. The way the G.I.s felt about the English families who were so hospitable to them is summed up in a letter received by Mr. and Mrs. White from a G.I. called Rudy:

"Dear Mr. and Mrs. White,

You must have guessed that both William and I shipped out of Pheasey when you didn't see us at the dance Monday night, I was sorry to have to leave after I had begun to like the people and the estate, but such is the army and these things can't be helped. I'm taking a chance on your address because, as you can see from the envelope, I only know the number of your house, but I hope it reaches you anyway.

It certainly was nice of you to accept us so readily and treating us so friendly. I appreciated your hospitality and shall not forget it. I hope some day I can repay you - my first real friends in England. Thanks ever so much for making this strange country feel more like home. Mr. White, being an ex soldier, must know how one feels in new surroundings so he can understand my sentiments. I really enjoyed those 'after midnight' conversations and that never failing 'cup of tea'. As for you, Mrs. White, I shall never forget that you were the first English girl that I enjoyed dancing with. I'm sincere when I say that without a doubt you even surpass some of our own girls from the States, and I'm not pulling your leg.

Well, thanks for everything, and I would love to hear from you in your spare time. Cheerio folks and Good Luck,

Sincerely Rudy."

CHAPTER 11
The Wash House

The contract for the laundry of the servicemen at Pheasey Camp was held by Harris's Dry Cleaners on the Aldridge Road. Even so many G.I.s approached local women on the estate to carry out this service for them.

Vera Stanley remembers a group of rather muddy G.I.s coming to her door to ask the whereabouts of a local laundry. She readily agreed to wash and iron their clothes. She recalls that the uniforms were made of a superior material to that of the uniforms of the British servicemen:

"Their socks were nylon and the uniforms were made of lovely material, fawn and brown, not like our soldiers in rough khaki and brass buttons."

Vera's aunt lived two doors away and her house became known as 'the Wash House'. She kept five tubs in the back yard which were always full of soaking clothes. Many of the G.I.s left items in their pockets so she would leave these in a pile for the men to sort out when they collected their things.

Emily Matts, who lived in Raeburn Road, also washed and ironed for the G.I.s. She remembers being surprised at how fastidious the Americans were about their appearance as up to this point she had thought them quite slovenly in their dress. She recalls being asked to press box pleats in their tunics. As she was busy with her own household tasks she limited her washing and ironing service to a small number of servicemen but even so she found that on numerous occasions she was still ironing at 12 0'clock at night in order to complete the work.

Patrick Wagstaff remembers that the children would often collect the washing for their parents and that the Americans paid well for the service. G.I. Bill Beatty recalls that a week's wash cost him half a crown. Edna Baker recalls:

"All the neighbours used to do their washing for them, they paid us very well bringing cookies and cigarettes."

Beatty Jones also did laundry for the Americans. She recalls that ;

"It gave us a nice little supplementary income"

She recalls that several of the G.I.s for whom she washed and ironed came to her house in the evening to pay social calls, bringing with them items of food. One sergeant, known as Tex, worked in the cookhouse and regularly brought tins of spam, fruit and coffee plus the occasional bag of sugar. The Americans would often have supper at Beatty's house and then play a game of cards which invariably lasted well into the night despite the curfew.

Phyllis Baker remembers that on some occasions G.I.s were given orders to move out with very little prior warning. This meant that clothes had to be collected from the ladies who were washing them quickly. Some were still in the process of being laundered and had to be returned unironed or even wet.

Edna Baker remembers that often the servicemen who had to leave at short notice had to abandon the items that were still in the wash, therefore the ladies who provided the service often inherited an assortment of G.I. clothing. Bill Beatty recalls that he was one of the men who had to retrieve his clothes at short notice when his moving orders came.

Stella Davies remembers being approached by a G.I. on her way home from shopping with her daughter, Angela one day. The man asked if she had an iron and ironing board he could borrow. She answered in the affirmative and led him to her house. Once she had handed him the iron and board he proceeded to set up the board and plug in the iron. As he only appeared to have the clothes he had on with him she was a little concerned as she asked him what he wanted to iron. When he answered 'my pants' she thought that he was about to take his trousers off but instead he reached inside his tunic and produced a spare pair of trousers and ironed them.

The local housewives not only took in laundry for the G.I.s, they also let those who had no running water in their billets use their bathrooms. Mrs. Brant remembers G.I.s knocking at the door to ask housewives to run errands down to the local shops or sew buttons on for half a crown. Pat Simmons remembers that her mother, Mary Green, would often take in sewing for the G.I.s.

Roland White, who was previously a tailor, used to offer to alter G.I. uniforms to a better fit and so became known as the 'camp tailor'. Earl Lovelace remembers his first meeting with Roland. Earl went to a boxing match at the Community Centre where he stood next to 'a friendly English man'. He recalls:

"We talked and he noticed that my G.I. jacket was too big for me. He told me he was a tailor and would take my jacket home, cut it down and have it back before the boxing matches were over. I didn't know what to do, that was the only jacket I had but I took him to be honest. He had a piece of chalk and marked the sleeves, shoulders, arms etc. He was back in time and my jacket fitted well. We became friends and I went to his house and met his wife and small boys."

Terry, one of those small boys, recalls that his father also made garrison caps from old jackets. He remembers the time that a G.I. called on the family in the early hours of the morning. On this occasion Terry was sleeping in one of the downstairs rooms of the house when the front door opened and an officer walked in asking for the 'camp tailor'. Terry told him that his father was in bed so the American went upstairs and knocked on Roland's door. Roland was not pleased about being woken up so early in the morning but he calmed down when the officer explained that he had recently arrived at the base and he hadn't realised that the White's house wasn't part of the camp.

Not all of the residents were so helpful. Some of them weren't averse to making a profit from the temporary residents. Fourteen year old Bernard Slim, who used to help the local milkman, remembers that the milkman would often sell spare bottles of milk

NOT FOR THE WOUNDED

HOW ABSENTEE SOLDIER GOT GOODS BY FRAUD

FROM U.S. ARMY CAMP

Stated to have been an absentee from his regiment since July 13, because, by his own account, he was not allowed to go to France, Pte. James Bibey (20), whose home address is 8, Wyndam Street, Treherbert, Rhondda Valley, Glamorganshire was charged at Aldridge Police Court on Monday with obtaining by false pretences, and with intent to defraud, from Pte. Ruben Kaprielian at a Midland U. S. Army Camp on September 12, three packets of biscuits and one bar of chocolate valued at 1s, 3d., also with obtaining by false pretences from Major Burton Reece Cole five packets of cigarettes and two bars of chocolate valued at 1s. 3d. Defendant who was wearing sergeant's stripes first elected to be tried by jury, but after an explanation had been given to him he elected to be dealt with by the magistrates.

Second Lieut. Edwin Raymond Koelsch of the U.S. Army said that in consequence of a report, he went to the officers' quarters where he saw defendant who had three brown paper shopping bags which contained cigarettes, cigars, oranges and other articles. When witness asked him for an explanation he replied that he was collecting the articles for the British wounded in hospital. When asked what authority he had to collect the articles he replied that he could not produce any. The police were then called for.

Police-constable Faulkner who was called to the camp said that accused told him that he was collecting articles for British wounded soldiers at Marston Green Hospital. On the way to the Police Station after being arrested he told witness that he was an absentee and that his rank was that of private.

"On the Run"

He later made a statement in which he said that in July of this year he escaped whilst awaiting a court-martial. He went to Birmingham where he met a Corporal whose name he did not remember, and who was also 'on the run." They chummed-up and made friends with American soldiers. They were told that there was a camp in the district and decided to' go there and ask for articles on the pretence that they were for the wounded. They sold some of the articles at public houses in Birmingham to poor class people. On the morning of the offence he did not meet his friend so he went to the camp alone. The articles they had sold the previous night made £2 10s. 0d.

Witness added that the articles accused had in the carrier bags were valued at £3 in American money, which meant that they were worth about £20 in British money.

It was stated that defendant was a native of Wales. His mother was dead and he had nothing to do with his step-father.

Defendant, who told the magistrates he was very anxious to serve overseas, was fined £3 for false pretences, the other charges being taken into consideration. He was remanded in custody to await an escort, the presiding magistrate (Mr. I. Green) observing that he thought the Army authorities would grant the man's wish to serve overseas.

BOUGHT FROM U.S. SOLDIER

WALSALL MAN HAD 700 RAZOR BLADES & OTHER ARTICLES

A PUBLIC-HOUSE DEAL

Having pleaded not guilty at Walsall Magistrates' Court on Wednesday to buying from an American soldier 730 razor blades, two tooth brushes, and a convalescent jacket, of the total value of £2 2s., issued for the use of soldiers and the property of the United States Army, William Hathaway (34), labourer, 17, Whateley Road, was granted legal aid and Mr. C. L. Hodgkinson appeared for him.

Detective-sergeant Warner stated that he went to Hathaway's house with a search warrant and informed prisoner that he had reason to believe that he was in possession of American Red Cross property. Hathaway replied "Carry on, you will find nothing here," but he found 700 razor blades and a tooth brush in a cardboard box, 30 more blades and another tooth brush in a jacket pocket, and the convalescent jacket in a sideboard drawer. Hathaway then said that he bought the blades from a "Yank" in a public house in Park Street for 10s., but he did not know anything about the tooth brushes.

Bought Pig in Poke

Giving evidence, Hathaway said the American soldier told him he had some articles in a cardboard box which were his own property and he was willing to sell them. He (prisoner) told him he had only 15s., and the soldier at first said they were worth more than that, but later sold them to him for that sum. He did not know exactly what there was in the box, except that there were some razor blades, nor did he know that he was doing wrong.

Mr. Hodgkinson submitted that there was no indication on the articles that they belonged to the U.S. Army, but the magistrates (Mrs. Dewsbury and Messrs. A. W. Cotterell, J. J. McShane and G. R. Hamson) found the case proved.

The Deputy Chief Constable (Superintendent T. Raybould) then informed them that Hathaway had six children the eldest of whom was aged ten years and that he had not worked for several months owing to ill health. He was in receipt of 19s. a week national health insurance and £3 5s. from the Social Welfare Committee.

"You have committed a serious offence, for which you could be sent to prison and you go into a public house and spend money given to you for your wife and children," the Chairman told prisoner. In consideration of his circumstances, however, the magistrates had decided to deal leniently with him, and he would be bound over for two years.

Walsall Observer 23/09/44   *Walsall Observer 19/05/45*

to the servicemen, pushing them through the boundary fence on the Queslett Road. He would charge the Americans two shillings (10p) for a 4d (2p) bottle of milk. Harry Baker remembers becoming friendly with an American known as 'Whiskey Bill' who would often ask Harry to get some whiskey from the pub. This Harry would do, charging a percentage on top of the normal price.

The Walsall Observer relates an account of a trial that took place at Aldridge Police Court regarding an incident at Pheasey in September 1944. Private James Bibey was charged with:

" - - - obtaining by false pretenses and with intent to defraud from Private Reuben Kapnelian at a Midland U.S. Army camp on September 12th 1944 three packets of biscuits and one bar of chocolate valued at 1s 3d, also with obtaining by false pretenses from Major Burton Reece Cole five packets of cigarettes and two bars of chocolate valued at 1s 3d." *

Apparently two British deserters had met in Birmingham where they made the acquaintance of some American soldiers from Pheasey. On learning the whereabouts of the camp they: - - -

" - - - decided to go there and ask for articles on the pretence they were for the wounded." *

Second Lieutenant Edwin Koelsh caught Private Bibey red handed in the officers' quarters at Pheasey with three shopping bags full of cigarettes, cigars, oranges and other items. Private Bibey explained that he was collecting the items for the British wounded at Marston Green Hospital. Lieutenant Koelsh called in the police when he found that Bibey had no documents to support his story. Apparently the articles in the bags were worth £20 on the black market and Bibey and his accomplice were planning to sell the items in Birmingham pubs to 'poor class people'.

On the morning of the offence Private Bibey, who was wearing sergeant stripes, visited the camp alone. When asked the name of the corporal, he said that he couldn't remember. Private Bibey, who was from Glamorganshire in Wales, explained that he had deserted because he hadn't been allowed to go to France to fight.

The court decided to fine Private Bibey £3 for false pretences. He was remanded in custody to await an escort so that he could be taken back to his unit to be court martialled for desertion. The presiding magistrate observed that:

" - - - he thought that the Army authorities would grant the man's wish to serve overseas." *

In May 1945 the Walsall Observer tells of a Walsall man who was convicted of being in possession of American Red Cross property. Several G.I. issue items were found in his house, namely razor blades, U.S. Army toothbrushes and a convalescent jacket. When the police arrived to search his house apparently he told them:

"Carry on, you will find nothing here." *

But eventually he did admit to knowing about the razors and confessed that he had brought all 730 of them from a 'Yank' in a public House in Park Street for ten shillings.

Walsall Observer.

Hathaway said that the American soldier had told him that the razor blades were his own to sell and pleaded that he did not realise that he was doing anything wrong.

Not surprisingly the magistrates did not believe Hathaway and found him guilty but when they heard that he had six children, the oldest of which was only 10 and that he was unemployed because of poor health they decided to deal leniently with him and he was bound over for two years.

The chairman of the magistrates did make the point to Hathaway that:

" *You have committed a serious offence for which you could be sent to prison and you go into a public house and spend money given to you for your wife and children."*

Some of the G.I.s were not averse to selling some of their issued equipment for profit to themselves. Harry Austin remembers the Americans selling army blankets at bargain prices. Bob Webb remembers that G.I.s would often negotiate for fresh eggs and vegetables with the local residents. In return the Americans would produce tins of fruit of various types, also tins of instant coffee which were a novelty in England.

The majority of the people living on or around the estate were happy to help the Americans out in anyway they could, not just for the financial remuneration but because these young men were far away from their own families and they had come so far to fight alongside the British servicemen who were the sons, brothers, husbands and fathers of those who were living on the estate.

On the whole the G.I.s were generous and happy to pay back any favours done for them. Iris Sidaway writes:

"They were just plain generous to a fault. I would never accept gifts from them even though they were my dear friends, I wanted them to know that I liked them for what they were, not what they had. I liked them for their warmth and kindness which they gave to anyone who accepted it."

CHAPTER 12
Aladdin's Cave

On the whole children of the estate and the surrounding area accepted the presence of the Americans. They had none of the preconceptions of their parents. Some of them did not even remember the area as it was before their arrival and did not perceive them as being newcomers or outsiders. Eleven year old Harry Turner would go out of his way to cross paths with servicemen from Pheasey. He recalls the sight that he must have looked at the time:

"- - - with a tatty old jumper, short trousers and well worn socks hanging around the tops of my old Daily Mail boots. Other lads around my age from Dulwich Road, on a Sunday afternoon would walk across to the Odeon, Kingstanding and up to the Deers Leap Public House which was opposite the end of the American soldier's base. On our way we would pass many G.I.s making their way towards Kingstanding Circle and the Odeon. The call was always the same: 'Got any gum chum?'

A favourite activity of the local children was to roam around the various areas of the Pheasey camp which were accessible to the civilian population and also some parts that were not so accessible. Harry remembers crawling through the hawthorn hedge which divided the fields in the Doe Bank Lane area. He and his friends would then run with heads ducked to the far side of the camp rubbish tip where the G.I.s wouldn't be able to see them. He recalls:

"'Look what I've found', someone would shout and this was repeated by us all at some time or another. Chocolate, candy bars, gum, part empty packets of cigarette, the odd tin of fruit. If we found an American army badge that was really special - - - surprisingly really the things that were thrown away that we were only too eager to find. On our way back to Dulwich Road with overflowing pockets and stuffed jumpers we had to dodge the bigger and older lads because they were sure to take our goodies from us. This seemed to be our Sunday afternoon out."

Harry Ashford also remembers visiting the dump regularly. He and his friend, David Pinner, would also spend time scavenging through the discarded items before they were covered over. Some of the items he found, such as knives, forks and spoons, he is still using today, more than fifty years later. He remembers that a Sergeant O'Brien, armed with a revolver, used to patrol the dump at regular intervals.

Other children went to the camp to visit the Americans themselves. Thirteen year old Dennis Flynn recalls:

"Most of the lads from the part of Kingstanding close to the camp would visit from time to time. My pal and I would pay them a visit, we would have a chat with them and watch them carry out their rifle drills and physical training."

Bob Webb remembers that the soldiers would play various ball games with the children in their off duty periods and Patrick Wagstaff remembers that the American cooks would give cakes and leftovers to the children who waited outside the cookhouse. He also recalls that the men would dress the children up in uniforms and then give them rides around the camp in jeeps.

Dennis Flynn was invited to visit the P.X. at the camp. He recalls:

"It was like Aladdin's Cave, some of the items I hadn't seen for three years."

G.I. Bill Beatty notes in a letter to his family:

"The children nearby have sort of invaded our area and ask us for American coins, candy, chewing gum etc. - - - and cigarettes, supposedly for their papas but not always."

Dennis Flynn had commenced smoking at the age of ten in 1939. By the time he was thirteen he was smoking five Park Drive a day. As he recalls:

"When the G.I.s came over I was able to widen my choice and went up market with such famous names as Lucky Strike, Fifth Avenue and Camel to name a few."

He remembers that the soldiers would often offer him a cigarette and sometimes tell him to keep the pack.

Alan Price was not so grateful to the G.I.s for giving him cigarettes. He attended the Grammar School in Walsall and he remembers that the Americans often used their playing fields for drill and P.T. and that they used to give the boys Camel cigarettes when the teachers were out of sight. Alan recalls:

"After a few puffs the smell and taste was most obnoxious to lads having their first smoke. we came to the conclusion that this cigarette was made from camel dung."

On the whole the American servicemen were generous to the children that they met. They were mindful of the deprivations that they were suffering because of the war and the rationing situation. and tried to give them some treats. Edna Baker remembers that one G.I. who came to visit her, built a swing in the garden for her three year old, Linda. He also took Linda to the Christmas parties which were held for the children of the estate in the Community Centre theatre hall.

The Christmas parties were the highlight of the year for the children on the estate. Terry Westwood remembers them vividly:

"The tables would be laid in the large hall packed with all sorts of food such as I had never seen before. After the party the hall would be cleared and rows of chairs placed in the hall, the screens would open up and we were treated to an hour of cartoons and adventure films wonderful to most kids who had never seen a 'real cinema'. As we left we were given a large paper bag full of sweets and games to bring home."

Ten year old Patty Green was also invited to the parties at the Community Centre. She lived at 26, Pomeroy Road and opposite her house was a piece of waste ground known as 'Pomeroy Sandcliffs'. On this the soldiers had built a small platform out of bits of wood. Patty and her friend would sing and dance on this platform for the G.I.s. Pat remembers singing 'The Chocolate Soldier from the U.S.A.' and Ma, I Miss Your

Apple Pie'. Around twenty soldiers would watch the girls perform. One of these men, Bill Beatty, wrote home to his family about Patty:

"Last night a little girl of ten years old came up the hill and the boys started talking to her - or I suppose she started first. She entertained us for about two hours talking a blue streak and singing. She could sing just about everything from Ave Maria to Yankee Doodle Dandy. She was a really smart kid - talked like an adult and knew just about everything we could ask her - difference between Irish, Scottish and English people, how they liked Americans etc. - a real rosebud from Ireland. By the time she left she had everything from candy and pennies to a rosary and crucifix - we got her to sing by giving her something."

Pat remembers that she never went short of sweets and chocolate. In fact her mother would melt some of the chocolate with hot water to make a bedtime drink for her. She also remembers the occasion when the men clubbed together to raise nine pounds which they gave to Pat's mother to buy a bike. Pat remembers going with her mother to Knightons in Kingstanding to buy it, it had 26inch wheels and she was very proud of it as it was the first bike she had ever had.

Many of the local children had cause to be grateful to the G.I.s. The men would often empty out their pockets for them, giving them coins (English and American) and, of course, gum or candy. Vic Tims remembers tagging along behind the soldiers at

Bob Webb at Raeburn Rd 1940's (Bob Webb)

Reunion of Pat Simmons (nee Green) right and Bill Beatty 1998 (Bob Webb)

every opportunity, hoping to receive some handouts. On Sundays Terry Westwood and his friends would sit on the embankment on the Queslett Road to watch the G.I.s parading. As they marched along they would throw out chewing gum and sweets to the children. Lou Lewis remembers that the Americans would often sit on top of the wall of the large circular water tank located on the Kingstanding Road. From here they would throw coins and gum to the ground and watch the children scrambling for them.

Joyce Ongley remembers the occasion that an American truck passed her and her friends as she walked to school along the Kings Road. As the truck passed her the tailboard became unhinged and some of the contents fell out. The vehicle stopped to let one of the men pick them up and as he did he opened one of the tins which contained peaches to offer to the girls. Being unsure of how to react the girls politely refused as they resumed their journey to school.

Doreen Garner remembers that one particular soldier was very generous to her and her family . Doreen, who used to live in Kings Road, was ten or eleven when the G.I.s arrived at Pheasey. She recalls:

"One day I was playing in the road, as we always did, and I had learnt to whistle with my fingers in my mouth. This American soldier came up to me and asked me if I would teach him how to do it. I said I would and proceeded to give him instructions. He passed my house on the way to the Circle, where the Kingstanding Pub was, every evening, so each evening he would have a lesson. After about three weeks he started to whistle quite well. He was really excited about it. He became friends with my family and used to bring food parcels to the house."

The children on the estate attended Raeburn Road Primary School, now Pheasey Park Farm Primary School. The temporary school which opened on April 13th 1942 was reached by a dirt path that ran from Raeburn Road. Either side of the path was flanked by long grass and poppies. The school, which consisted at the time of a number of prefabs, had a wire mesh fence separating it from the back gardens of the surrounding houses. These houses were used to billet G.I.s

Terry White remembers that:

"there had been an order given that no G.I. was to give candy to the children as it was causing a nuisance, and it was thought dangerous because children were running alongside lorries shouting: 'Got any gum chum?' One morning two of us were walking to school. Two G.I.s were walking in the opposite direction but behind the fence. When they had passed us we heard a whistle and turned around to find them walking on, but on the fence was a pile of K. rations and candy."

Terry Westwood also attended Raeburn Road school. He used to look forward to playtime. He recalls:

"Every playtime G.I.s came down to the fence to pass candy bars and chewing gum through the wire to the waiting kids. This would be immediately confiscated by the teachers when we got back to class. For anyone actually caught receiving in this way the punishment was quite harsh. On the occasion that I was caught the teacher

walloped me with the blackboard ruler."

Terry regrets that he never actually tasted any gum as it was either confiscated by his teachers or his parents. He remembers one school day when he was particularly grateful to a couple of G.I.s. He recalls:

"My mother allowed me to go to school on my scooter. One day I accidentally rode over a girl's coat. She had put it on the ground to do some handstands up the school wall. The girl immediately burst into tears and told the teacher. In vain I protested it an accident and was dispatched with the girl to her house to apologise to her mother for my terrible crime.

"On leaving the girl's house I realised that I had no idea where I was. Scooting my scooter around various roads I became even more lost and finally sat down on the kerb sobbing. Around the corner came an American jeep, picked me up, gave me some gum and took me back to school where my mother was frantically waiting. The G.I.s calmed down my mother and took both of us back to Crome Road where the neighbours were in total awe of us getting out of an American jeep."

Although accepting sweets from the American soldiers was not tolerated by the staff at Raeburn Road School, the Americans did make the effort to promote good relations between themselves and the school. On 18 April 1944 the men put on a concert for school funds. The school records state that the grand total of £11-10s was raised which was enough to purchase a gramophone.

At 13, Dennis Flynn was attending Aldridge Road School. He recalls that:

"It wasn't difficult to pick out the kids from Kingstanding in the playground at Aldridge Road School, most of them were dressed in service men's clothing (apart from the greatcoat)."

The children received items for their families, as well as themselves. Sylvia Brown remembers that some asked for nylons and chocolates for their mothers. Bob Webb remembers gratefully receiving anything off the G.I.s that had market value or could be useful for swopping like sweets, Hershey chocolate bars, decks of playing cards, spare badges and buttons from uniforms and British and American coins.

Parents often warned their children not to talk to the G.I.s but these warnings were usually ignored. Stella Davies remembers telling her four year old daughter, Angela, not to tell any of the American soldiers that her father was away from home. On almost the first occasion that Angela spoke to a G.I. over the fence at the top of her garden she blurted out:

"My Daddy's away in the army you know."

Seven year old Sylvia Brown, who lived in Kingstanding, remembers her friends teaching her to say: 'Got any gum chum?'. She and her friends would jump on the bus, talk to the G.I.s and then jump off again, or simply stand at the bus stop waiting for the buses with Americans aboard to stop so that they could shout out their requests. When they saw the children the G.I.s would throw out the contents of their pockets to them. Sylvia knew that her mother would have been horrified if she had known what she was doing.

Similarly Keith O'Duffin remembers that when the G.I.s gave him gum:

"We had to eat it without my mother seeing it as she thought it a horrible habit. When Frank, my sister Joan's guy, gave us gum I would hide the wrappers behind the gas fire in the front room and when years later Mom had that removed she discovered my secret and said: 'I knew you were eating gum. I could never find the wrappers, but you weren't able to hide the smell.

The children's parents also disapproved of the 'balloons' that the G.I.s gave to the children. Ron Crisp remembers the Americans sitting on the wall outside the Collingwood Centre giving these out to any children who should pass by. When they got home the 'balloons' were confiscated by their parents who could see that they were actually condoms.

Many of the children were happy to run errands for the G.I.s, particularly if the Americans were going to pay them. The Children would often be asked to fetch fish and chips and sometimes beer from the 'outdoor' at the pub.

Doreen Green, whose parents ran a hardware store on Kings Road, remembers her parents being puzzled when they sold out of the galvanised steel and white enamelled buckets. They soon found out that the Americans were buying the buckets so that they could give them to the local children to fetch chips for them.

Keith O'Duffin recalls that when the Americans asked the children to fetch them fish and chips from Kingstanding Circle: - - -

" - - - they always gave us far too much money and I'm afraid lots of the lads ripped them off. I didn't because I had a sister who went out with one of the officers - - - so when I turned up at the camp with plenty of fish and chips and plenty of change the guys were very pleased."

Jean Phillips recalls that the children would often charge the G.I.s a pound for chips that cost just two shillings. Patrick Wagstaff remembers that the Americans often confused the ten shilling and the one pound note and that he and his friends would take advantage of this. Bob Webb comments that:

"As the G.I.s became more familiar with the U.K. currency the profit margins of the local kids diminished."

Several of the local children thought up other enterprising ideas to make some extra pocket money from the Americans. Doreen Garner used to collect flowers from her front garden and make them into bunches to sell to the G.I.s for their girlfriends.

Stanley Minchin used to collect the empty beer bottles from the large public air raid shelter near the Old Horns Pub. One penny was paid for the return of each bottle. As air raids were infrequent after 1944 the shelter was often used by courting couples. Stanley would often find army penknives on the floor that had been used to open the bottles of beer and then dropped. These penknives could either be sold by Stan or bartered amongst friends for other items.

Thirteen year old Bernard Slim was a newspaper delivery boy for Richards the news agents near the Deers Leap at weekends and school holidays in 1944. He had two rounds, the second one encompassing the north-eastern side of the camp. Front doors were rarely closed during the day so Bernard would go into each house and shout 'papers' at which point G.I.s would appear to buy a paper. They wouldn't always have the correct money on them, so Bernard would get to keep the change. By the end of the round his pockets would also contain gum, candy and fruit. Bernard's favourite part of the round would be the kitchens and Mess Hall in Gainsborough Crescent. Here he would be given doughnuts and packets of soup and, on one occasion, part of a turkey carcass.

G.I. James Brady remembers that some of the local children would come to the back doors of the houses with loaves to sell to the soldiers:

"Many of us debated every time meal time rolled around as to whether or not the chow was worth the puffing and sweating entailed in climbing the hill to the Mess Hall. Often times the lethargical elements of our intellects won out and we stayed behind in the rooms munching our P.X rations or the loaves of bread the little British urchins used to sell at our doorstep." *

James recalls the time when there was a spot inspection of one of the sergeant's billets and he was caught red handed with a loaf of bread:

"- - - pressed unceremoniously onto a clothes rack." *

Not all of the Americans welcomed the advances of the local children. Harry Turner recalls that some used to get fed up with 'Got any gum chum?' As he says:

Post Exchange Pheasey (10th Replacement Depot Archives)

Invasion Post Office – James Brady.

"All the kids were at it."

Lou Lewis remembers that:

"Quite often the Yanks used to emerge from the pub in a drunken state requesting us kids to guide them through the fog to the Pheasey Camp, the bus service long since finished. As we guided the Yanks up to Pheasey they would often hand us money, gum or other items as a reward for guiding them through the fog.

"However not all the G.I.s were so appreciative of our help. Some were quite abusive after drinking and cursed the lousy English weather and the 'Damn Limey Kids'. On rare occasions like that we kids realised that the chances of us being rewarded for our assistance were pretty slim therefore we decided to even the score at the earliest opportunity.

"The route to Pheasey took us via Kingstanding Circle. The island, approximately 50 -60 yards in diameter was bordered by a paved footpath around its circumference. As we made our way through the murky fog someone amongst us hatched out a prank to play. On reaching the Circle we led the drunken G.I.s onto a pavement encircling the island. Having deposited them there we left them with the advice: 'O.K. Yanks, just keep following the pavement and it will take you right to Pheasey.' How long they walked in circles is anyone's guess!"

For the majority the relationship between the children and the G.I.s was a good one. Terry Westwood reminisces: ·

"My personal memories of the G.I.s were very happy ones bearing in mind that most kids accepted them as always living there as we did not know any different."

He believes that youngsters were attracted to the G.I.s as they:

" - - - spoke and dressed differently and always seemed very happy, they did not seem to have the drab look that our parents seemed to have. Not understanding the word 'war' and what it entailed we were happy in our innocence."

CHAPTER 13

Brief Encounters

The Americans at Pheasey were not averse to using their good relationships with the younger children of the area to get in the good books of their older sisters. Eleven year old Joyce Ongley remembers sitting on her garden fence in Wandsworth Road, Kingstanding when a G.I. came up to her to ask if her older sister, Dorothy was about. Joyce ran to get her seventeen year old sister who looked out of the window to see who the G.I. was and promptly told Joyce to get rid of him.

Jean Bridgeman remembers a G.I. asking her about her fifteen year old sister, also named Dorothy. The young man gave Jean a box of chocolates to give her sister in return for a 'date'. Naively Jean, who had no idea what a 'date' was, relayed the message to her sister. When her father heard he was furious and forbade Dorothy to meet the man.

Hilda White, nee Quirk, met and started courting G.I. Fred Whitman at a dance. Fred was not particularly good at dancing so the couple spent subsequent dates at the cinema on Kingstanding Circle. Occasionally, when Fred had K.P. duties he would be late to pick Hilda up but he always ensured that he got Hilda home by 10.00.p.m. when she had to be in.

Eventually Fred asked Hilda to marry him but she was very close to her parents and couldn't contemplate going to America. Fred continued to write to Hilda when he was sent overseas and intended to return to England to spend some time with her at the end of the war before he returned to America but by this time Hilda had met her future husband, Bill, so she didn't reply to Fred's letters.

Mary Biggs, nee Merryweather, has a similar tale to tell:

"I was out for a stroll one Sunday afternoon in October when two G.I.s came walking towards me. They stopped and asked me how to get to Walsall, but not being very familiar with the town, I couldn't help them. They seemed to want to talk, I think they were feeling rather lonely. I was eager to talk too as I had an uncle, aunt and cousins in America and they were very interested. I invited them home to meet my parents and my grandmother who was delighted. They made themselves quite at home, one was named Arvil Weimer from Frankfurt, West Virginia, the other was Charles from Charleston.

"During the evening they asked where they could go for a drink so I took them to the Kingstanding Pub on the Circle. It was packed with G.I.s but we managed to get a seat. Arvil seemed to take a shine to me and his friend, Charles, decided to leave us alone. I never saw him again. Arvil insisted on seeing me home although he would be late back to the camp.

"He asked me to meet him again the following Tuesday. I waited at the bus stop

on the Circle for about an hour but he didn't turn up so I went back home thinking: 'Well, that's that.' Three days later I had a postcard from Glasgow saying that he was sorry to have missed me that night and that he would write to me as soon as he could. I found out later that he had been sent to Iceland but of course he couldn't tell me at the time.

"Some months passed then I had a letter from him. He said he was feeling fed up and wished the war was over. He asked me to send a photo, which I did. I had about three letters from him which I still have and the postcard and also a photo of him taken in France. Then the letters stopped so after a while I came to the conclusion that I wouldn't see or hear from him again. By then I had met my future husband, a Brummie like myself. We worked together at the same factory. We planned to get married in August 1945.

"One night, in April of that year, I had been working late and I arrived home around 8.30.p.m. My grandmother was on the front step looking for me. She was very excited. I went in and there was Arvil sitting in the armchair. I just could not believe it, he hadn't forgotten me. He was back at Pheasey Camp for a few days before going overseas. I told him I was getting married and he said: 'He's a lucky guy.'

"I felt awful, he was such a nice, well mannered young man. After all that time (nearly two years) he'd found his way back. I walked back with him to the Circle bus stop as he had to get back to the camp. He wished me all the best for the future and his last words to me were: 'Take it easy.'

Arvil Weimer somewhere in France (Mary Biggs)

Jack Crowley (S. McGlade)

"I had been married a couple of weeks when I had the last letter from him. He was back in England, in hospital, he had severe frostbite, it had been a long winter in '44 and '45 in Germany and the Americans were in the thick of it. - - - I wonder if he ever thinks about his time in Kingstanding. It really was a 'Brief Encounter.'

Beryl Clarke also enjoyed a 'brief encounter' with G.I. Michael Palumbo. Beryl met Michael at a dance at Kingstanding Community Centre in 1944. Beryl was 16 years old and had gone to the dance with her friend, Mary. After that night Beryl and Michael regularly met at the dances and also went to the Odeon on Kingstanding Circle, after which they would buy a fish and chip supper from the fish shop in Kettlehouse Road. Beryl particularly enjoyed attending the dances with Michael as he was an accomplished drummer and would often get up on the stage to play drums with the band.

Eventually Beryl took Michael home to meet her family. They were a little concerned to find that Michael, at 26, was ten years older than their daughter but they still welcomed him into their home. He repaid their welcome by bringing tins of fruit, candy, chewing gum and cigarettes for the family.

After a few weeks Michael was sent over to the Continent and he and Beryl kept in touch with letters. Shortly after the war ended in 1945 Beryl received a letter from Michael informing her that he would be coming back to England and would like to visit her. Pleased at the prospect she arranged for him to stay with her parents and they made the most of their time together. During this time Michael asked Beryl to return to America with him so that they could get married. Beryl had mixed feelings and

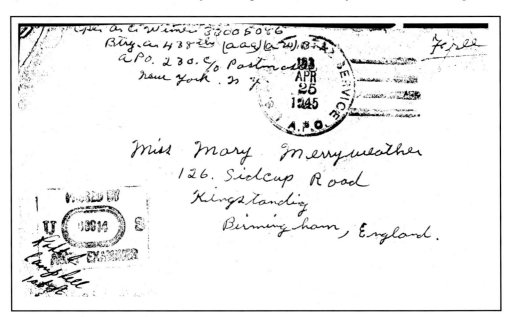

Letter sent to Mary Merryweather from Arvil Weimer

couldn't decide what to do. She was very fond of Michael but felt that leaving home would be too big a wrench for her particularly as returning home to visit friends and family would be almost impossible once she arrived in the States.

When the time came for Michael to leave the matter was still unresolved. He returned to America and was discharged from the army. The two corresponded until 1949, Michael continually asking Beryl to come over to the States to marry him and offering to pay towards the boat fare. Finally it was Beryl's father who decided the matter as he declared that if Michael wanted to marry Beryl he would have to return to England. After this the letters became less frequent until they stopped altogether.

A number of girls who had been dating G.I.s did not hear from them again once they had been sent to the Continent. One local girl went out with Sergeant J. Doyle of 3004 Ordnance Company. She recalls:

" - - - we had a great time together in the short time that I knew him."

He was suddenly shipped over to France and she received a Christmas greetings card and photograph dated February 1945. He also sent two of his colleagues to visit her but she never heard anything from him again. She reminisces:

"I still have the photo and greetings and my memories of him."

Lily Ross also lost touch with her boyfriend when he was shipped out of Pheasey. She met Jack Crowley at the Masque Ballroom which was situated just off the Stratford Road. Lily had been forewarned by her mother about the Americans and had

Beryl Clarke (B. Clarke)

Pfc Michael Palumbo
3rd Inf Division (B. Clarke)

been advised not to be taken in by their flashy gifts, big talk and casual chat up lines. Lily had no intention of meeting any Americans and avoided the big dance halls in Birmingham city centre where many of them congregated.

One particular night in late 1944 she intended to go to the pictures with her girl friend but another friend, Violet, persuaded her to go dancing instead. Once there Violet's boyfriend, who was in the R.A.F., unexpectedly turned up and Lily was left sitting at the table by herself.

As she sat there she noticed an American serviceman enter the dance hall and as she looked up she caught his eye. Embarrassed she quickly looked down again but he came over to ask her to dance. Lily loved dancing but soon found that her partner had two left feet. To her relief at the end of the dance he suggested that they sit the next one out. They chatted and she found out that Jack was based at Pheasey Farms Replacement Depot. He was a sergeant in the 35th Infantry Division and he had been serving in France when a land mine had exploded nearby shattering both his eardrums. For a while he had been almost completely deaf. After the dance Jack walked Lily home and then asked her to help him sort out his bus fare money, which she did.

The next night Lily went to her local pub, The Belgrade, with her neighbours and this is where Jack found her. Lily was surprised as she didn't expect to see him again. Apparently Jack had tried to remember her address and had only knocked on one wrong door before finding Lily's house where her mother had directed him to the pub.

From this time on the romance between Lily and Jack developed. He was well liked in the close knit neighbourhood, he often brought gum with him for the local children. Lily remembers that he would always politely drink every drop of the coffee her mother specially prepared for him as she knew that Americans didn't drink tea. Afterwards he would tell Lily that the drink bore no resemblance to American coffee.

The romance ended abruptly one Thursday evening in May 1945 when Jack failed to turn up for a date. Lily was worried as he'd never missed a date before. She thought that he must have been moved out from Pheasey but no letter carrying an explanation arrived either. Lilly's worries increased when she found out that she was pregnant.

Dreading her mother's reaction Lily went to her aunt for help. Aunt Slim took Lily to the camp at Pheasey but when they got there they found that it was empty of all but a handful of men who were responsible for closing it down. In desperation Lily's aunt took her to the American Red Cross Club in Birmingham. Lily, cringing with embarrassment, pretended to faint on the step so that she wouldn't have to go inside. At the Red Cross Club they told her that it was not their policy to trace and inform fathers as there were many girls in Birmingham in the same situation as her. They did offer to find a home for her baby but Lily had no intention of giving the baby up and went back to her everyday life hoping that Jack would get in touch. When he didn't she presumed him dead.

On September 17, 1945 Shirley was born in Lily's home in Long Street. Later, when she found out the facts surrounding her birth Shirley took it upon herself to trace her father. In May 1987, after 15 years of searching Shirley traced him and found that he was still alive. Unfortunately he remembered nothing of his time in Birmingham and his relationship with Shirley's mother. Shirley was able to fly to America to meet her father. He acknowledged her as his daughter and gave permission for her to add the appendix to her birth certificate: 'Father's name - Jack Crowley'. Lily had similar physical features to Jack and they found that they had much in common but Jack never regained his memory of his time in Birmingham.

Seventeen year old Cicely Jeremy met Herman Craven from Kansas City in Missouri in November 1943 as she was returning home from the cinema. As she stepped out into the blackout she tripped over and dropped her handbag and the contents spilt all over the ground. As she bent to pick up the items she heard an American voice ask if he could help. She thanked him and together they picked everything up.

Herman, known as Hank, insisted on walking Cicely home and so she asked him in for coffee. Her parents made him very welcome and he soon made himself comfortable in front of their fire. He was in no hurry to return to Pheasey where the G.I.s had ripped out and burnt every cupboard and floorboard to keep warm.

From this time the Jeremys became Hank's second family and he spent all his leaves at their house. Cicely's younger brother and Hank's sister became penfriends and even their parents started writing to each other. Their fathers were both veterans of World War One so they had something in common. Hank's family sent food parcels

One of the G.I.'s who visited Deer Leap Pub, known only as Bob

Bill Farley (Joyce Ongley)

of ham, fruit and sweets to the Jeremys. The day a tin of sweetcorn arrived there was great excitement as it was the first one the Jeremys had seen.

Although Hank and Cicely spent a lot of time together and became good friends they did not fall in love. Hank already had a girlfriend, Margie, back home and Cicely had fallen for a G.I. she had met earlier who was now serving overseas. It wasn't long before Hank was sent to France. The couple wrote for a while but then the letters stopped and they lost touch with each other.

In 1988 Cicely was surprised to receive a letter from Hank. Apparently after watching a programme about England he had decided that he would like to contact his British family. Unfortunately Cicely's parents had died by this time but she arranged to travel to the States to meet Hank with her 36 year old daughter, Elizabeth.

Cicely had some misgivings about meeting up with Hank after all this time but these soon disappeared when she met him and his wife, Margie, at the airport. The members of the two families got on well together, particularly Elizabeth and Hank's son, Chris. A week before Elizabeth was due to return home Chris proposed to her and she accepted. The wedding took place five months later at Hank's home. After the wedding the couple moved to England to be near Cicely. Cicely has become Chris's second mother, taking on the role that her mother played to Hank for the period that he was based at Pheasey.

Long distance love affairs were not easy to conduct and there were several reasons why relationships between local girls and G.I.s from Pheasey did not stand the test of time. Sometimes it would be the fault of the girl who would meet someone else or her family who would insist that the relationship be ended. Sometimes the American would find that he lost his ardour once some miles had been put between the girl and himself. Sometimes the G.I. had a girlfriend, or even a wife, back in the States that he hadn't told the English girl about, or, in some circumstances, the G.I. was wounded or even killed in combat while fighting on the continent.

CHAPTER 14

Romantic about Coalsmoke

Not all of the romances that started between G.I.s from Pheasey and English girls ended so abruptly. Several girls from the area met and fell in love with Americans and eventually got married. The local newspapers announced a number of weddings involving G.I.s from Pheasey.

Twenty two year old Albert Eisenkraft entered the U.S. Army in December 1942. At basic training in Texas he was tested for proficiency in the German language (which was the language spoken at home during his childhood) and was accepted for further training. In early 1944 Albert was assigned to the Military Intelligence Training Centre in Maryland. By July 1944 his training had been completed.

The majority of Albert's fellow graduates had been born in Germany and spoke fluent German with a German accent, however Albert spoke with an American accent and could not pass for a native German so he was assigned to the Military Intelligence Service where his duties would include interrogating and interpreting for prisoners of war.

In early October 1944 Albert and 200 of his colleagues were shipped to Glasgow by convoy in a tramp steamer. Albert sums up the trip:

"What a trip - seasick, lousy food, enormous cockroaches, ongoing poker games, submarine scares. As a child of the Depression I had never travelled too far from New York City, so being sent all over the U.S.A. and then overseas was quite an experience."

From Glasgow the group travelled by train to Great Barr Station where they found trucks waiting to take them to Pheasey Farms.

Albert's Military Intelligence unit was only assigned to Pheasey for a fortnight but Albert remembers that they:-

"- - - were treated quite differently from others who come before us. We were, after all, a bunch of German speaking people, many with pronounced German accents."

Fortunately Albert was not unpopular with everyone that he met. He recalls:

"The second night at Pheasey (and in England) a companion, Murray, and I went to the American Red Cross Club in New Street. We had a sausage and mash dinner and listened to piano music played by a lovely red head. She was joined by a friend who caught my eye and my friend and I introduced ourselves. Elsie Hogg was the friend, and I fell in love there and then."

Elsie clearly remembers the evening. At that time she was a civilian electrician at Cosford Aerodrome. She maintained Spitfires, Whitley Bombers and gliders and also flew on test flights to check her work. She usually left home, Leonard Road in Handsworth, each morning at 5:30 a.m. and returned at 6:30 p.m. unless she stopped off to see her friend, Vicki Barnes, (the piano player) or if there was an air raid.

Elsie had been engaged to a young man in the R.A.F. for the past four years. He was stationed in Egypt and had broke off the engagement to marry a nurse over there. When Elsie met Albert she didn't know what to expect. She recalls:

"I had heard many rumours of the G.I.s - none good- but a friend of mine asked if I had been out with any and I said 'No'. His reply was: 'Then you should give them a chance.'"

Albert and Murray asked the two girls to show them Birmingham. Elsie continues the story:

Blackout made that impossible but we said we would have one drink with them before we went home. This we did and I invited Albert to my house if he wished to visit. Next day he arrived in the evening and we spent a pleasant evening just talking. I wasn't sure what to make of him - his uniform greatcoat was miles too big for him but he was well spoken. He came the next evening and he informed my mother he was going to marry me and she said : 'What did you say your name was - Crazykraft?!'"

Albert visited Elsie every evening. He was aware that Elsie's mother thought him mad and suspected that Elsie thought he was too but he recalls:

"With my need to see Elsie I spent as little time at Pheasey as possible."

Some time during this period Elsie received a telegram stating that Albert was in the U.S. military hospital in Lichfield so that weekend she made the journey over to visit him, after spending a few anxious days wondering why he had been hospitalised.

American Red Cross Club, New Street Birmingham (C. Hinde)

Once in the hospital Elsie remembers having to walk down a long corridor with beds either side full of wounded soldiers. By the time she got to Al her face was crimson with embarrassment as she had been wolf whistled all the way down the corridor. To her relief she found that Al had been hospitalised with nothing more serious than the flu.

Once Al had recovered he was sent back to Pheasey and one day later he was shipped overseas to France. Al recalls his anguish as he left Elsie in November 1944 fully expecting never to see her again.

Al's unit were issued jeeps and in groups of four (two per jeep) drove to Southampton to embark for Lehavre. In France, just south of Paris, two officers joined the group and after an evening in Paris they drove to the Bastogne in Belgium to interrogate German Prisoners of War at Corps Headquarters. From there the group travelled to Luxembourg and then Schlausenfach, a small town in Germany, where the men were assigned to the 106th Infantry Division. Albert and two of his colleagues were assigned to the 422nd regiment.

During the course of the battle the 106th Division were overrun. Albert's team of three was captured on December 19th while the members of the other team were killed. Albert was detained until late March 1945 at Stalag 9B (a sergeant's camp).

Although Al wasn't a practising Jew he was of Jewish descent. Towards the end of his time in the prison camp the Jewish P.O.W.s were lined up. Albert presumes that the intention was to shoot them but fortunately news of the impending arrival of Patton's

Elsie Hogg (A. Eisenkraft)   *Al Eisenkraft, 1944 (A. Eisenkraft)*

Third Army prevented the German guards from carrying out the execution.

As the Allied troops moved nearer to the prison camp the prisoners were assembled to march out of the compound. When the guards tried to move the men from Stalag 9B they found the British and Commonwealth troops cooperative lining up smartly and marching out - many to their death as Allied planes strafed the lines of marching men, thinking them to be Axis troops. Knowing this would be the case the American prisoners decided on a plan of passive resistance. They refused to line up and wandered around the compound in a disordered fashion. Each man had saved a sliver of soap from Red Cross parcels they had received while in the prison camp, so, at a given signal, they placed these under their tongues and immediately started frothing at the mouth. The other prisoners were instructed to carry them to the side and leave them there, which they did. Shortly after this the camp was liberated by the Third U.S. Army.

Both Albert's family in the States and Elsie in England had been notified that Albert was 'Missing In Action' and had no idea that he was alive until April 1945. Although Elsie had had her letters returned with 'Missing In Action' stamped on them she retained the hope that Al was still alive. During this anxious time she started writing to Albert's mother and his sister, Gretchen. Albert continues the story:

"I was back home in mid April 1945 and after a home leave I was sent to a 'rehabilitation camp' - a fancy hotel in Lake Placid, New York for three months. I was 95lbs in weight when freed, 65lbs less than my usual weight at that time.

English Girl Flies Atlantic To Wed Former War Prisoner

Elsie Hogg of Birmingham, England, flew the Atlantic to become the bride of former Sergeant Albert E. Eisenkraft of South Ozone Park, a war prisoner in Germany for five months.

The couple met while the bridegroom was stationed in England.

The ceremony took place in the Jamaica Presbyterian Church with the Rev. Donald W. Ruth officiating.

A reception followed at the home of the bridegroom's sister, Mrs. Al-Ian Hendricks of New Milford, N. J.

Arlene Whitman was maid of honor, and the best man was Victor Murray, both of Jamaica.

Ushers were Clinton Bleg of New Hyde Park and Andrew J. Nolte of Brooklyn.

The bride, daughter of Mrs. Elsie Hogg of Birmingham, went to school in England. She has been a secretary.

Mr. Eisenkraft, son of Mrs. J. H. Eisenkraft of 135-11 109th avenue, is a graduate of New York University School of Commerce and belongs to the University Club and the Young Men's Board of Trade. In the Army Intelligence, he was captured during the Battle of the Bulge.

The couple are making their home at the South Ozone Park address.

American Red Cross Club (C. Hinde)   *Long Island Daily Press 27/5/46*

"After the Army had decided that all my 'nuts and bolts' were in place I was assigned to teach English and Democracy to a selected screened group of German P.O.W.s in the U.S. on an island in the bay of Newport, Rhode Island. During that time I bombarded Elsie with telegrams and letters pleading with her to marry me."

In October 1945 Elsie agreed to marry him. Albert sent an engagement ring over in the post but Elsie refused to pay the customs the large amount they wanted so it was sent back. In October Elsie phoned Pan Am for a flight but was told to phone back in January of the following year. On 1st January she phoned again and was given a seat on the first flight available which was May 15th 1946. At that time the journey was taken by D.C.6 in stages, stopping at Dublin, Newfoundland, and New York. The entire trip took two days. Elsie recalls the flight:

"I had a good flight over as I sat next to an older American businessman who told me what to expect and about New York in general. We were delayed overnight at the old airport in Newfoundland and the next day we had to make an emergency landing at Connecticut where I spoke to newspaper and radio reporters who asked me some questions."

In her handbag Elsie had the money for her return fare in case she didn't like what she found in America.

Once in Connecticut it was necessary to catch a bus to New York City which

Al and Elsie Eisenkraft
(A. Eisenkraft)

Al and Elsie Eisenkraft in recent years
(A. Eisenkraft)

arrived at 10 p.m. on May 16th. she met Albert here and was finally able to receive and wear her engagement ring.

Elsie was to stay at the Presbyterian Manse with the minister and his wife, Don and Betty Ruth, for the week prior to her wedding day. This couple were to become Elsie's life long friends. She recalls:

"Betty took me to the stores to food shop and I was overwhelmed by the quantities of fruit - bananas, apples, oranges, grapefruit, pineapple, grapes, and amazing (to me) cereals, breads and, on a visit to a bakery store, cream cakes (real cream), fruit cakes, coffee cakes, cream doughnuts etc. When asked what I would like I said: 'One of each.' Butter and meat were rationed but not like I was used to and the local butcher was extremely kind to me as were most people."

The couple were married in the Presbyterian Church of Jamaica, Long Island, New York. Elsie wore her sister's wedding dress that her mother had made. After the wedding Albert and Elsie spent some time with the Ruths. Albert's mother was ill with cancer at the time and died July 1946.

At first Elsie was homesick so she got a job in the office of a paint and wallpaper store so that she could save for a visit home. It took until 1948 to save enough for the fare but then she sailed on the Queen Mary for a three month visit to England.

When she arrived in England she smelt the smog and understood what Al meant when he had told her that he felt 'romantic about coalsmoke'. It was the smell he associated with England where he met his bride to be. After two weeks in England with motherly intuition Mrs. Hogg said to Elsie:

" You'd go home tomorrow wouldn't you?"

Elsie stayed the three months and then sailed home on the Queen Elizabeth. Once back in America it didn't take long to settle into her adoptive country. She recalls:

"I made friends very quickly and the young couples group at church took us under their wings. I loved the 'League of Nations' I found with all the nationalities of people in our area. I really loved, and still do, New York City. It is a whole 'other world' "

Mrs. Hogg and Elsie's sister, Edith, were able to visit the couple for six months in 1949. Albert remembers buying an old car and fixing it up so that he could take the Hogg family on a trip to Niagara Falls. Following this Elsie planned a trip back to England every two years with Albert occasionally accompanying her when his work allowed.

Elsie is now an American citizen although she retains her British citizenship too. At this point the couple have been married for fifty three years. They have two children and a granddaughter. As Elsie comments:

"We are well blessed. Our daughter says: 'We will be a hard act to follow.' "

CHAPTER 15
Two English Roses

Nineteen year old Pat Capasso arrived in Great Britain on 19th December 1943. He had sailed over on the Queen Elizabeth from New York Harbour to Greenock in Scotland. After coming ashore he and his companions were taken to the rail station where they boarded a train to Lichfield. A number of the men Pat was with were assigned to the 10th Replacement Depot at Whittington. The rest, including Pat, were sent to Pheasey. Pat remembers his arrival at the camp at about 3 a.m. in the morning. It was pitch black and extremely cold.

As part of the Christmas festivities a dance had been organised at the Collingwood Centre soon after Pat's arrival. Pat decided to go along as he had nothing better to do. Inside the hall a small band was playing on the stage and the dance hall was full of G.I.s and girls. Pat noticed three attractive girls standing together. He introduced himself to them and found that they were sisters who were with one of the local firms who had hired a coach for employees and friends to attend the dance. The girl's names were Ann, Mary, and Rose Field. It was Rose that Pat felt an instant rapport with.

During the course of the evening Pat found that Rose was a bus conductress employed by the Midland Red Bus Company on the Sutton Coldfield to Birmingham

Pat Capasso somewhere in France
(P. Capasso)

Pat Capasso in insignia of the
101st A.B. Division (P. Capasso)

route. Previous to this she had worked at I.C.I. on munitions work but it had been necessary to leave because she developed an allergy to the working conditions there.

Shortly after the dance Pat visited Rose at her home in College Road, Erdington, where he met her parents and her other two sisters, Helen and Grace. Although Rose's parents were always polite and welcoming to Pat they had some reservations about their daughter dating an American soldier.

Like Al Eisenkraft Pat was only stationed at Pheasey for a couple of weeks but during this time he saw Rose as much as possible. The couple would often take long walks, calling in at various of the local pubs. They also went to the Odeon Cinema on Kingstanding Circle. Rose would sometimes have to work when Pat had off duty time so Pat would spend the time travelling on Rose's bus between Sutton Coldfield and Birmingham so that he could at least be spending the time with her.

Towards the end of January 1944, with very little warning, or time to say goodbye, Pat was given orders to move out from Pheasey. Pat and another G.I. were sent to a camp at Pencoed, South Wales where they underwent combat training. In late February Pat was sent to a camp near Reading where he was assigned to the 101st Airborne Division. Later he took part in the D-Day landings. During this time Pat and Rose kept in touch by letter. Because of security restrictions Rose never knew the exact location of the camps Pat was stationed at. She used an A.P.O. number which served as an address. At the end of the war Pat applied for leave to return to England to marry Rose. As Pheasey Camp had closed down by this time Pat stayed with the

Pat Capasso revisiting Pheasey 22/5/99 (R. Webb)

Pat and Rose Capasso (P. Capasso)

Pat and Rose Capasso (P. Capasso)

Munroes, neighbours of the Field family.

Pat and Rose were married on 22nd August 1945 at St. Lukes Church, Kingstanding. Pat's best man was a colleague from the 101st Airborne Division, Johnie Musselman Jnr. Three of Rose's sisters, Ann, Mary and Grace were her bridesmaids. The couple had a brief honeymoon in the Cotswolds before Pat had to return to his unit and Rose returned home to her parents.

Pat was discharged from the army on his return to the States on 7th December 1945. Early in 1946 Rose travelled to Tidworth Barracks, Salisbury Plain, for processing as a G.I. bride. From there she sailed on the E.B. Alexander, arriving in New York in March 1946.

Looking back Pat reminisces:

"It took me sometime to realise what she had left and what she was getting into. It could not have been easy. She was very homesick. After four years or so I had to take her home with our daughter, Rosanne, who was two and a half years old at the time. After a few months in England It relieved some of her homesickness and she began getting used to the American way of life. We visited England quite often after that."

Sadly Rose passed away in 1987.

John Carpenter arrived at Pheasey in early April 1944. He was in his mid twenties at this time. For some time previous to this he had been attempting to enlist in the army, but as a boy John had lost the index finger of his right hand in a farming accident and consequently had been rejected by the army three times on medical grounds. When he was finally accepted he commented:

"I don't know how the war effort was going but they must have been getting pretty desperate for men of any shape or size, with or without fingers!"

John sailed on the Queen Mary from New York to Greenock. From there he travelled by train to Great Barr (now Hamstead) Station. From the station he and the other G.I.s were transported by truck to Pheasey.

John spent his off duty time at Pheasey exploring the area around the camp. Instead of turning towards Birmingham and the city life he decided to look around the farms in the local area as he himself came from a farming background. John was billeted in a house in Stanhope Way, so from there he made his way along Doe Bank Lane in the direction of Barr Beacon. He eventually came upon a local farmer repairing fencing at the boundary of his land and Doe Bank Lane.

The farmer was Jim Wright who had been farming Beacon Dairy Farm since 1937. The farmhouse, which had been built in 1934, was owned by the Cadbury family. The Wrights were to be tenants until 1957 when they bought the land from the Cadburys.

After talking for a while Jim invited John up to the farmhouse to meet his family. On arriving at the farmhouse John was introduced to Jim's wife, two daughters, Rose and Mary, and son, Jim. The family were surprised that Jim had brought a G.I. to the

John and Rose Carpenter (J. Carpenter)

John and Rose Carpenter leaving the church (J. Carpenter)

house as up to that point he had not shown any interest in the soldiers at the camp.

From that time onwards John spent virtually all of his off duty time at the farm helping out with the milking and other chores and also playing cards with the family. He built up a close relationship with Jim, and also with Rose, the older sister. Jim would often lend John his civilian work clothes so that he could work comfortably and also so that he would not be recognised if any of the M.P.s called at the farm to find out if any of the men were 'off limits.' John often stayed at the farm after curfew and on numerous occasions Jim would help him to re-enter the camp unobserved and without being apprehended by the Military Police or guards.*

Eventually John became regarded as one of the family. They did not realise that he had more than a passing interest in Rose. Rose herself saw John as 'just another G.I.' She explains:

"We really never had dates as such, the only places we really went to were a concert at Birmingham Town Hall or a show at one of the theatres. Jim always came with us."

At the beginning of June 1944, after spending two months at Pheasey, John was shipped out to Portsmouth. A few days after D-Day he was sent across the channel to France. During the 21 months that John was in Europe he wrote to Rose and the Wright family as much as possible. Rose recalls:

"We did not hear from him for some time then I began to receive letters, lots of them."

John returned to England at the beginning of March 1946 to propose to Rose who accepted. John duly approached Jim Senior to ask his permission. Jim's answer was to ask what John would do if he said no to which John replied that he would go ahead and marry her anyway.

John Carpenter and Jim Wright on the farm (J. Carpenter)

* See Chapter 4

John managed to obtain a 30 day leave to get married. He stayed with Mr. and Mrs. Morris (friends of the Wrights) in Moreland Road the day before the wedding which was set for Wednesday March 20th 1946. The wedding had to be on a Wednesday as this was the only day milk rounds and other chores on the farm allowed. Rose remembers the date as:

"The first day of Spring, a very, very happy day."

The wedding took place at St. Margaret's Church, Great Barr with Jim Jnr. as John's best man. Rose's dress was simple, plain and long. She remembers that because of the rationing situation it was quite a feat to get enough clothing coupons to clothe herself and her two bridesmaids but her friends helped her out.

When John arrived at the church he was surprised to see the large number of people there so he told the friend who was driving to carry on as he must be at the wrong church. Since then Rose has always teased him that he got cold feet and was looking for a way out.

The reception was held at the Wright's farmhouse and was attended by family and close friends. Rose and her sister made the cake. It was a three tier fruit cake complete with marzipan and icing. Rose recalls that:

"In spite of rationing we put on a decent meal. Raising pigs we always managed to have a ham on hand, also chicken and eggs. Mother was quite a cook. Looking back it was amazing what we managed to put together."

Rose Carpenter's bridesmaids
(J. Carpenter)

John and Rose Carpenter
(J. Carpenter)

After the reception John and Rose went away to London for a few days for their honeymoon. Their main reason for choosing London was to meet with the Red Cross to register Rose's trip to America as a G.I. bride. The couple sorted through the paperwork with a Red Cross Girl. By chance it happened that she had attended the University of New Hampshire, which was just four miles from John's home. When the girl realised this she became more friendly and as Rose says:

"From then on it was plain sailing for us."

After getting everything settled for Rose's journey to the U.S. John returned to his unit in France. He was discharged from the army in April and he sailed from Lehavre to the States on the 30th of that month. He landed in New York in May.

Meanwhile Rose did not need to go to Tidworth to have her papers processed because all the paperwork had been completed in London. She travelled down to Southampton and sailed from there on the John Ericsson. Once on board ship she was given an information sheet that set out the rules and regulations for the crossing. This included instructions on smoking:

"Do not throw lighted cigarettes overboard as they can easily be blown back into the ship."

It also gave instructions on electrical appliances:

"The electrical current on this ship is unusually high - 230 volts D.C. - - - therefore no personal pressing irons, curlers or other electrical appliances will be plugged in cabins or wash places. To do so will almost certainly cause short circuits and fires."

The ship produced a daily newsletter called 'The Seaweed Gazette' which gave information about the ship radio station, W.J.E. The brides took it in turns to be announcers. There was obviously plenty to do on the ten day voyage. The Gazette gave a list of films that would be shown at the ship cinema and on one particular evening thanked the brides for leaving the cinema quietly, not waking the children who were sleeping nearby. The gazette also announced the venue and times for bingo and the whereabouts of a library and an office from where games such as chess, cards and dominoes could be borrowed.

There was also a nursery for the children on board furnished with toys, play pens and trained staff. A unit of army nurses were on hand to take care of the health of the brides and their children. They no doubt found their new duties very different to the ones they had a year earlier working in tented hospitals near to the battle lines.

While on board the brides could attend a series of lectures that would introduce them to life in the States. These included titles such as : 'An Introduction to the U.S.;' 'American History;' 'American Government;' 'Naturalization;' 'Preparation of Food and Cooking a la American Style;' and 'Fashions in America.'

On May 30th the John Ericsson docked in New York Harbour where John was waiting to meet Rose. It was necessary to pay a small fee as the brides came ashore. Later John was to comment:

"Just think for ten bob I could have had my pick of thousands"

Rose quickly settled down in America. She reminisces:

"I was truly made to feel very welcome by family and friends. Guess I had moments. The only real bad one was the first Christmas. That was a very tough day for me - but I survived."

The couple have now been married 54 years and as Rose says:

"I can honestly say I have not regretted one minute. Three great kids, seven wonderful grandchildren. What more can one ask for out of life?"

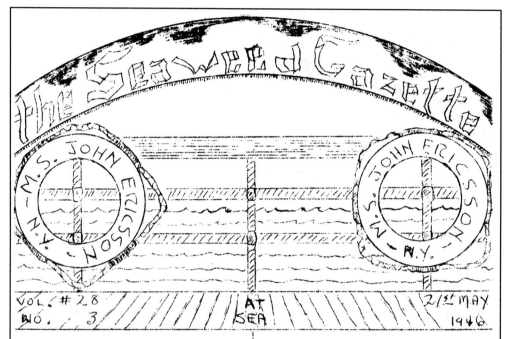

STATION WJE IS ON THE AIR -

Today makes the third day that those words have heralded the best in sweet and swing music entertainment. The battle between the top crooners and the top orchestras is waxing hot and interest is picking up. Bing Crosby leads the crooners with Frank Sinatra, Dick Haymes, Perry Como and Andy Russell following in that order. The late Major Glenn Miller's orchestra holds down the number one spot there followed by Tommy Dorsey, Jimmy Dorsey, Harry James, Sammy Kaye, Charlie Spivak and Les Brown. Suggestions have been rolling in for what people want to hear and many more requests are anticipated.

THROUGH SICKNESS AND THROUGH HEALTH -

And we hope that the only time you'll meet any of the swell gang of nurses aboard will be while you are in a healthy condition (not that we doubt their abilities as nurses, but they are wonderful people to meet while not so sick). Just in case you do insist on getting seasick or have trouble with your formula making or get any other kind of illness - then they'll assist you or nurse you back to health.

Captain Margaret E. Blatt is the Principal Chief Nurse and rides herd on her flock of twelve nurses. Capt. Blatt's home is Freedom, Pennsylvania.

Seaweed Gazette-Magazine given to Rose Carpenter aboard the M.S. John Ericson (Rose Carpenter)

CHAPTER 16
The Most Wonderful Man in the World

Master Sergeant Marvin Wallman came over to Great Britain in January 1944 on the Empress of Russia. Previous to this he had spent two years in Iceland as Company Clerk and Chief Clerk for Company C. of the 2nd U.S. Infantry Division. Marvin travelled with a group who were on 'rotation' to England arriving at the Firth of Forth in Scotland a week later. From here he was assigned to bases in Bristol, Chard, Wolverhampton, Lichfield and then to Pheasey.

While in Wolverhampton awaiting reassignment Marvin met Coralie Kendrick in a pub. He remembers walking into the pub and seeing a group of five people, four of them were obviously in couples, but he was surprised to see that the one he considered to be best looking was sitting by herself. Coralie also clearly remembers the occasion when she first met Marvin. She writes:

"I met Marvin in a dimly lit pub while the blackouts were still in force. I knew immediately when he spoke that he was intelligent and modest. We were unable to spend much time together as the pubs closed at 10 p.m. We had already missed the last train so Marvin and his colleague insisted that my friend and I take the taxi with them and since there was only one taxi we had to sit on their laps. I really did not know until the next night much about Marvin, only that he was tall and slim and everything about him was just right."

Coralie lived in Wednesbury and was the youngest of seven, having four older sisters and two older brothers. She worked for the L.M.S. Railway, first at Great Barr Station then later at Dudley Port.

After that first night the couple spent as much time as possible together. One day in May the two were walking together along the street when Marvin simply asked:

"Will you come to America with me?"

Coralie's Answer was 'yes' even though she had only known Marvin for two months. Marvin needed to get permission to marry from the military so, as part of the process, Coralie was visited by an army chaplain who, to her surprise, tried to arrange a date with her. With hindsight Marvin wonders if this may have been a test to see if she was really serious about marrying him. If it was a test Coralie passed it as at the end of the interview the chaplain explained that he was only there to ensure that mistakes were not made on either side and that he was happy for the marriage to take place.

On 15th June 1944 Marvin was assigned to Pheasey Camp (via Whittington Barracks). He describes his duties and his memories of the camp:

"I was in charge of a small group of about 15 men which directed some of the incoming and outgoing troops. We directed them to digs and found them the necessary articles of bedding. I remember that the humidity there was so bad that I could not

light my pipe, so on sunny days I spread my tobacco on the window sill so the heat could dry it. The billet was a small two storey 'row house'. It was comfortable enough. I remember very little of the camp itself as I spent my spare time cycling to Wednesbury."

Marvin and Coralie were married on 3rd August at the Parish Church in Wednesbury. Marvin's best man was his serviceman friend, Fred Tiff. Coralie recalls the morning clearly:

"When I awoke I looked out of the window, it was overcast and drizzling but I did not care. It was my wedding day and I was marrying the most wonderful man in the world and about to take an adventure for the rest of my life."

The couple didn't let the weather dampen the occasion and after the wedding they held a party. Marvin managed to get two 24 hour passes so that he could remain away from Pheasey until the following day.

Marvin stayed at Pheasey for the first three weeks after the couple were married. They made the most of weekend passes to travel to London and Stratford Upon Avon and to visit Coralie's relatives. Coralie recalls that:

"Three weeks after we were married I received a telephone call from Marvin. He was being transferred to Bromborough (in Cheshire) and some of the men were being shipped overseas. He did not know if he would be one of them or not and he asked me if I would be willing to go to Bromborough on a chance that we would be able to see each other. I called my sister and asked her what I should do (She had lost her

Marvin and Coralie's wedding (M. Wallman)

William Lang (I. Lang)

husband to pneumonia after being married just two and a half years.) and she gave me her advice - 'If it were my husband I would go.' She and I took time off work and she accompanied me to Bromborough. To my amazement I was able to see Marvin coming up the lane."

In Bromborough Marvin was assigned to the 504th Quartermaster Unit with four officers over him. Marvin comments:

"I have never seen four such useless people together either in or out of the army."

Marvin was only able to get overnight passes for two weeks. It was necessary for Coralie to visit the doctor twice to get a 'sick note' so that she could get the time off work. She recalls:

"The last night in Bromborough I kissed him goodbye, not knowing where my husband would be going to, or the next time I would see him."

From Bromborough Marvin's unit was sent to Southampton and then to France via Omaha Beach. After the battle of the Bulge he was sent to Oise (in France) where he was assigned to a unit carrying out administrative work. He recalls:

"One duty was to serve on a board which reviewed requests by soldiers to be returned to the United States because of unusually bad circumstances. This was allowed because the fighting was nearly over. After Hitler's death in May 1945 I put my own name down, not because of bad news but because I had been away for so long. I left France at the end of May and got ten days leave to spend with Coralie."

Marvin and Coralie's wedding (M. Wallman)

The couple spent some time together in England and then visited Scotland. Marvin flew home from Glasgow, arriving in Washington D.C. at the end of June. From there he took a three hour train ride home to Claremont, California, where his parents lived.

Coralie had to wait another six months to receive notice to join Marvin in the States. She travelled to Tidworth Barracks to be processed along with other G.I. brides

Travel Permit for Marvin to visit Coralie (M. Wallman)

W. Langs Identification card (I. Lang)

201– Wallman, Marvin J. (Enl)   1st W/Ind
Hq. 10th Reinforcement Depot, APO 874, U.S.Army.

TO: All Concerned.

    1. M/Sgt Marvin J. Wallman, 36205609 _____ has reported to this
depot per paragraph __2__, SO __5__, Hq. US Leave Area, NBS, APO 562
dated __25 May 1945__.

    2. In compliance with said orders, soldier is authorized delay en route
which will commence on ____30 May 1945____ at 0001 hours.

    3. M/Sgt Marvin J. Wallman, 36205609 _____ will report to this
headquarters for duty not later than 2400 hours, __6 June 1945__.

        For the Commanding Officer:

                JULES A. VICKNAIR,
                Captain, A.G.D.,
                Asst. Adjutant.

Pass for Marvin to visit Coralie before returning to the States (M. Wallman) then she finally sailed on the Queen Mary from Southampton to New York in February 1945. The voyage took six days. On reaching the U.S the American Red Cross helped Coralie to organise her journey across the country to California. Coralie recalls:

"I left my family, my mother, father, four sisters and two brothers on January 28 and arrived in San Bernardino, California on February 14, Valentine's Day, to see my wonderful husband waiting for me."

Coralie found her new home to be very different from her home in Wednesbury. Marvin recalls that she liked to sit on the porch of her new home and watch the orange pickers at work. She had new family and friends to get to know although she already felt at ease with Marvn's mother who she had been corresponding with for some time previous to her trip to the States. Both of Marvin's parents treated her like a daughter.

The couple still live in California. As Marvin says:

"Coralie has made me very happy and we have a lovely daughter, Gale, and two lovely and loving granddaughters, Tina and Sandy. Coralie is now 82 and still beautiful"

Twenty seven year old William Hamilton Lang came from Charlestown, Massachusetts. He was a truck driver. Like Marvin, Bill met his girlfriend at a pub, this time one close to the Gaumont Cinema in Steelhouse Lane, Birmingham.

Irene Smith, who lived in Beakes Street, Aston, with her two young children, Irene (aged 5½) and Roy (aged 4) had been widowed early in the war. Her husband, Herbert, had been one of the unfortunate men who was lost at Dunkirk. Irene was not told officially that her husband had been killed until 12 months later. At the time the War Department inferred that he may be a P.O.W. although Irene suspected that he had been killed when she did not hear from him after the events at Dunkirk.

In the meantime Irene and her young family had to be rehoused in November 1940 when a land mine landed near her house, causing damage to it. The family were temporarily rehoused in nearby Station Road before being returned to a house further down Beakes Street the following year.

In early 1944 Irene's eighteen year old niece visited her and suggested that she come with her to have a 'night on the town'. Irene decided that she had been in mourning for long enough and said that she would take up her niece's offer.

The couple visited a pub where they became engaged in conversation with Bill and his colleagues. Later in the evening Bill suggested that they go to the American Red Cross Club for a meal. After this Bill offered to escort the two girls back to their homes in Aston. Irene permitted Bill to come as far as the tram stop at Aston and then directed him to the tram stop where he could get transport back to Birmingham.

A couple of days later Irene answered a knock on the door to see Bill standing there. She wondered how he had found where she lived and Bill told her that he had remembered that she had said she worked for the Post Office so he had walked round the streets near the tram stop knocking on doors and asking if anyone knew where Irene Smith who worked for the Post Office lived. Eventually he was directed to

ENLISTED RECORD AND REPORT OF SEPARATION
HONORABLE DISCHARGE

1. LAST NAME - FIRST NAME - MIDDLE INITIAL	2. ARMY SERIAL NO.	3. GRADE	4. ARM OR SERVICE	5. COMPONENT
Lang William H.	3113459	P.F.C.	Air Corps	AUS

d. ORGANIZATION

Hq & Base Sv Sq, 442nd Air Sv Gp

7. DATE OF SEPARATION	8. PLACE OF SEPARATION
16 June 1946	AAF Giebelstadt, Germany

9. PERMANENT ADDRESS FOR MAILING PURPOSES

14 Arlington St. Summerville, Mass.

10. DATE OF BIRTH	11. PLACE OF BIRTH
31 July 1916	Charlestown, Mass.

12. ADDRESS FROM WHICH EMPLOYMENT WILL BE SOUGHT

13. COLOR EYES	14. COLOR HAIR	15. HEIGHT	16. WEIGHT	17. NO. DEPEND.
Blue	Brown	66 In.	139 lbs.	Two

18. RACE	19. MARITAL STATUS	20. U.S. CITIZEN	21. CIVILIAN OCCUPATION AND NO.
WHITE NEGRO OTHER (specify)	SINGLE MARRIED X OTHER (specify)	YES X NO	Truck Driver 345

MILITARY HISTORY

22. DATE OF INDUCTION	23. DATE OF ENLISTMENT	24. DATE OF ENTRY INTO ACTIVE SERVICE	25. PLACE OF ENTRY INTO SERVICE
17 June 1942	17 June 1942	17 June 1942	Fort Devens, Mass.

SELECTIVE SERVICE DATA ▷ **26. REGISTERED** YES X NO **27. LOCAL S.S. BOARD NO.**

28. COUNTY AND STATE	29. HOME ADDRESS AT TIME OF ENTRY INTO SERVICE
Charlestown, Mass.	16 Arlington St., Summerville

30. MILITARY OCCUPATIONAL SPECIALTY AND NO.	31. MILITARY QUALIFICATION AND DATE (i.e., infantry, aviation and marksmanship badges, etc.)
Auto Equipment Operator 345	None

32. BATTLES AND CAMPAIGNS

None

33. DECORATIONS AND CITATIONS

World War II Victory Medal, EAME Medal, Combat Badge, Germ Occup'l

34. WOUNDS RECEIVED IN ACTION

None

35. LATEST IMMUNIZATION DATES			36. SERVICE OUTSIDE CONTINENTAL U.S. AND RETURN		
SMALLPOX	TYPHOID	TETANUS	OTHER (specify)	DATE OF DEPARTURE	DESTINATION	DATE OF ARRIVAL
	5 Mar45	4 Feb45				

37. TOTAL LENGTH OF SERVICE						38. HIGHEST GRADE HELD
CONTINENTAL SERVICE			FOREIGN SERVICE			Private First Class
YEARS	MONTHS	DAYS	YEARS	MONTHS	DAYS	
0	1	15	3	10	15	

DATE OF DEPARTURE	DESTINATION	DATE OF ARRIVAL
2 Aug 1942	Liverpool, England	10 Aug 1942

39. PRIOR SERVICE

None

40. REASON AND AUTHORITY FOR SEPARATION

Convenience Of Government to enlist in RA. AR 615-365 and WD Cir 110.

41. SERVICE SCHOOLS ATTENDED	42. EDUCATION (Years)
None	Grammar 8 | High School | College

PAY DATA

43. LONGEVITY FOR PAY PURPOSES	44. MUSTERING OUT PAY		45. SOLDIER DEPOSIT	46. TRAVEL PAY	47. TOTAL AMOUNT, NAME OF DISBURSING OFFICER
YEARS 4 MONTHS 0 DAYS 0	TOTAL $300.	THIS PAYMENT $300.	None	None	$300. B. V. Hariss Maj. FD

INSURANCE NOTICE

IMPORTANT IF PREMIUM IS NOT PAID WHEN DUE OR WITHIN THIRTY-ONE DAYS THEREAFTER, INSURANCE WILL LAPSE. MAKE CHECKS OR MONEY ORDERS PAYABLE TO THE TREASURER OF THE U. S. AND FORWARD TO COLLECTIONS SUBDIVISION, VETERANS ADMINISTRATION, WASHINGTON 25, D. C.

KIND OF INSURANCE	49. HOW PAID			50. Effective Date of Allotment Discontinuance	51. Date of Next Premium Due (One month after 50)	52. PREMIUM DUE EACH MONTH	53. INTENTION OF VETERAN TO
Nat. Serv. U.S. Govt. None	Allotment	Direct to V.A. X				$6.68	Continue X | Continue Only | Discontinue

54.	55. REMARKS (This space for completion of above items or entry of other items specified in W. D. Directives)
	Honorably Discharged for convenience of government to enlist in the Regular Army. AR 615-365 and WD Cir 110. Discharged as Temporary Private First Class, AUS. Paid Enlistment Allowance of $150. by B.V.Hariss, Maj. FD

56. SIGNATURE OF PERSON BEING SEPARATED	57. PERSONNEL OFFICER (Type, name, grade and organization - signature)
William H Lang	*George J Hrico* George J. Hrico Capt AC 55th Fighter Group

WD AGO FORM 53-55
November 1944

This form supersedes all previous editions of WD GO Forms 53 and 55 for enlisted persons entitled to an Honorable Discharge, which will not be used after receipt of this revision.

William Langs Honorable Discharge document (I. Lang)

Irene's door. Irene felt that she had to ask Bill in as he had gone to such lengths to find her. Unfortunately as soon as he stepped inside the door her dog went for him.

After this the couple met as often as possible. Because of the nature of his assignment Bill was not able to see Irene as much as he would have liked. Sometimes he would call on her when he was travelling through the area. When Bill got off duty time he would often take Irene to the cinema or the pub. On other occasions he would spend time at Irene's house with her and the children. He was always reluctant to return to the camp after visiting and Irene remembers that he invariably returned to camp after the curfew and had to run the gauntlet of the M.P.s

The couple decided to get married so Bill went through the official channels and filled in much paperwork to get permission from the military. The wedding took place at St. Joseph's Church in Thimblemill Lane, Aston on 20th January 1945. Bill's best man was his friend, Sergeant Lester K. Zick. It was snowing on the day and Irene remembers her friends throwing snow over them in the absence of confetti.

In Spring Bill was posted to Europe but was allowed to return home for the birth of his baby daughter in July of that year. In June 1946 Bill was honorably discharged from the army. He immediately re-enlisted in the Regular Army as this would keep him in Europe. At the beginning of 1947 he returned to the States. He sent for Irene to join him but she was reluctant to do so as her son, Roy, was ill at the time.

Bill returned to Germany as part of the Occupation Forces and set about gaining a discharge so that he could re-enter the U.K. This would only be permitted if he had employment in England so it was necessary for Irene's family to find a job for Bill. It was in September 1947 that Bill was finally able to return to England and be reunited with his wife and two year old daughter, Wendy.

It took Bill some time to settle down into civilian life in England and he had several jobs before he settled into a job that he enjoyed, driving a lorry for Hardy Spicers in Erdington. Bill was popular at work where he was known as 'Yankee Bill' Sadly he developed a heart condition and died on February 10th 1974 aged 57.

CHAPTER 17
Pheasey Specials

Once it became known that there was an American camp on the outskirts of Birmingham, a number of 'ladies of easy virtue' from the surrounding area were drawn to the camp, attracted by the glamourous uniforms and free spending G.I.s. They were nicknamed the 'Pheasey Specials' by the residents of the estate. Several of these women appeared at Aldridge Magistrates Court charged with 'trespassing on military premises'. In one case Captain Szatkowsky was:

" – making a tour of the camp when he heard female voices in a room. He knocked upon the door and someone replied: 'Alright, keep your shirt on.' When the door was opened he saw three women in the room. He detained them and summoned the police.

"Police Constable Faulkner said that he went to the camp and arrested the defendants who said that they had got drunk the night before and found themselves at the camp. He conveyed them to the police station where they all gave wrong names and addresses. However the required information was later divulged by Plimmer (one of the girls) who also said that they had met some American soldiers in Birmingham and went to a public house where they had a lot to drink. The soldiers then took them to the camp in a taxi and stayed with them until the early hours of the morning." *

The Walsall Observer stated that twenty year old Olive Plimmer:

" – had been regarded as a respectable girl up to two years ago when she started to associate with American soldiers. - - - Plimmer's father said that he was willing to take his daughter on the understanding that she would stop at home and behave herself, which she agreed to do." *

She was placed on probation for two years while the other two girls were sentenced to three months imprisonment each. The chairman remarked that:

" – he was very sorry to see women in such a disgraceful position." *

Two months later there were more convictions at Aldridge Magistrates Court. This time all three girls were sentenced to three months imprisonment. Apparently in this case one of the girls had approached an officer from Pheasey to ask for his assistance in evicting her friend from one of the soldier's billets. When Lieutenant Skinner went to look he found the girl hiding in the closet in one of the rooms.

"Both defendants handed in written statements pleading with the magistrates to be lenient with them. Bate's husband said that his wife disappeared on November 3rd and he was not willing to have her back as it was the third time she had left him." *

The third girl was found in a locked room by a sergeant who was checking the rooms:

"When asked by the magistrate's clerk - - - what she had been doing during the last twelve months the defendant - - - replied that she did not wish to discuss the last

Walsall Observer.

twelve months." *

Frank Puttergill remembers arriving in Birmingham by train in the early hours of the morning when he was on leave from the R.A.F. To get back home to Pheasey it was necessary for him to wait outside Grey's Department Store in Bull Street for the Night Service bus. When it arrived, Frank was surprised at the number of G.I.s who filed out of the darkened doorways. The bus was soon full and Frank felt lucky to get a seat. When the bus arrived at the terminus at Pheasey, he was even more surprised to see the long queue of girls waiting to board the bus back into Birmingham and surmised that this must be the 'night shift' who had stayed over with boyfriends from the camp. This evening bus service also became known as the 'Pheasey Special' because of its occupants.

Terry White remembers the occasion when his family was on their way to the Trees. They stopped at Terry's aunt's house so that his mother could have a word with her. Terry recalls:

"Dad and I waited outside. An M.P. came around the corner and told my father to move on. Apparently there was a number of girls coming to the estate for the G.I.s and he had been told to move every one on. My father took exception to this saying that he lived there and would not move. Meanwhile a crowd of G.I.s had come out of the house at the top of Raeburn Road on the opposite side encouraging my father against the M.P. One of them shouted out: 'Where would you be if it wasn't for us?' That caused my father to go over the road. He was

WOMEN TRESPASSERS

ON LOCAL CAMPS FOR AMERICAN SOLDIERS.

Three more girls were convicted at Aldridge Magistrates' Court on Monday of trespassing on military premises in the occupation of U.S.A Forces. Defendants were Eileen Dorothy Bates (22), married and mother of two children, of 49, Top Street, Long Causeway, Farnworth, Rosina Miriam Johnson, (23), of no fixed abode, and Olive Hughes (24), 273, Heath Street, Winson Green, Birmingham. Upon being sentenced to three months' imprisonment each, Hughes collapsed in the dock and had to be carried out of court while Bates was lead out screaming.

In the case concerning Bates and Johnson 1st Lieut. Hugh Albert Skinner, of the U.S. Army said he was in the guard-room when defendant, Bates, asked him if he could help her in getting her girl friend (Johnson) out of one of the billets. He went to the billet. Two soldiers were in bed and Johnson was in a closet. The soldiers had already been dealt with.

Both defendants handed in written statements pleading with the magistrates to be lenient with them. Bates' husband said his wife disappeared on November 3, and he was not willing to have her back as it was the third time she had left him. About eight months ago he had to fetch her home from a London police station.

In the second case concerning Hughes, Sergeant John Lawrence Cashman of the U. S. Army said when checking billets he visited an upstairs room and found the door locked. A soldier said he had a girl inside.

When asked by the Magistrates' Clerk (Mr. Frank Cooper) what she had been doing during the last twelve months the defendant (Hughes) replied that she did not wish to discuss the last twelve months.

Walsall Observer 09/12/44

*Walsall Observer.

instantly surrounded. The M.P. got him out and we carried him to the Trees. When my father came out of the pub there was a squad of M.P.s and an officer waiting. He wanted my father to go back and point out whoever had shouted out but he wouldn't."

Some of the housewives who lived around the camp also played hostess to the G.I.s. Residents remember seeing G.I.s enter the front door of some of the houses on the estate after husbands had gone out to work on the night shift. In the morning as the husband came back from work through the front door the G.I. would leave by the back door. Ron Crisp recalls the occasion that a lady living near him was entertaining two G.I.s They had not been at the house very long when two M.P.s approached and banged on the door. As the two G.I.s were led away Ron heard them complaining:

"But what about our money, what about our bucks?"

Unfortunately this type of incident reflected on the other local women and many housewives felt that if they wanted to keep their reputation they needed to keep a respectable distance from the Americans. As Ray Smith remembers the cliché at the time was: 'Overpaid, oversexed and over here' and:

"Sadly the snap judgement was made that any young lady who befriended them was of loose morals"

There were also a small number of unpleasant incidents concerning drunken G.I.s forcing themselves on local women. These incidents were taken seriously by the officers at the camp. Tom Morrissey remembers that:

" – misbehaviour, especially toward women, was not easily dismissed. At the 10th Replacement Depot in Lichfield and at Pheasey we were lectured about maintaining good deportment with the English people. - - - I'm sure any reported offender suffered the horrors of the 'Lichfield Guard House', a real purgatory."

Mabel Cooke remembers the occasion when she accompanied her friend to the 'Outdoor' at the Trees to purchase a bottle of beer for her friend's husband. As they left the pub a group of drunken G.I.s emerged from the Trees and followed them. One attempted to assault Mabel's friend who hit him across the head with one of the bottles and rendered him unconscious. The girls hurried home to tell the friend's husband and he escorted them to the offices at the Community Centre to report it.

Fred Petragallo remembers having to take part in an identity parade while a woman, who claimed that she had been raped by one of the soldiers, attempted to identify the culprit. The men were ordered to stand in ranks and Fred remembers being very nervous although he was completely innocent. He knew that whoever the woman pointed out would automatically be considered to be guilty. At this time, a charge of rape carried the death penalty in the U.S. Army. Fred recalls that the woman was not able to identify the man.

Iris Sidaway recalls hearing of the reputation of the G.I.s and so she was very wary of them:

"Foolishly believing what people said I repeatedly turned down requests for a date from a young officer I had been introduced to. Then one day he said: 'We get on so

well, so why won't you come out with me?" and I answered, in my ignorance: 'Because I do not like the immoral reputation American soldiers have.' He smiled at me rather sadly and said: 'Don't you know that a woman will be treated with the respect she earns. If she doesn't earn it she won't get it. You, my dear, earn tremendous respect.' I accepted his invitation and spent many happy hours in his company until the day he left."

After this Iris dated a number of Americans and each treated her with respect. She remembers that if she refused a G.I.'s advances:

"They never took 'no' as an insult, they treated the whole incident as if your refusal was your right, they still continued to treat you as if you were the most precious thing in the whole world."

Iris concludes by commenting on the reputation that the American troops over here had by stating:

"A large portion of the blame must be on those girls who wanted to be used."

CHAPTER 18

From a Boy to a Man

The busiest time for Pheasey Farms functioning as a Replacement Depot was probably the beginning of 1944. This was the period when the Invasion Force was being built up in Britain. At the beginning of March 1944 the 4th Replacement Battalion had 314 enlisted men to train and process. By the end of March the Battalion had 1090 enlisted men as a large number of men were being sent from the States. At the beginning of April the Battalion historian, Sergeant Philip E. LeMaine wrote:

"At the time of this writing, which is 8th April 1944, morale in the Battalion is very high. The Battalion equipment is far from complete but at the rate it is arriving now it should be equipped, trained and ready to take to the field by 1st May 1944." *

At this point the soldiers arriving at Pheasey were generally unattached to units. From Pheasey they were sent to units where they were required. Usually only a few men were allocated to each unit. Before July 1944 it was unusual for a large group of men to be sent to one unit. The reverse was the case at Whittington where men were organised into 'packets' of about 200 men and then assigned to units.

The 769th M.P. Battalion was an exception to this rule at Pheasey. The whole of A Company was put on alert on April 27th 1944 and was sent to Bishopston, Bristol on May 2nd. As early as September 1943 the battalion had received equipment for teaching French to the enlisted men. As Lieutenant Giddings stated:

"Just a little foresight on someone's part in case we should take a little trip." +

In Bishopston the whole Battalion was reunited. The historian recorded:

"This was the first time the entire Battalion had been together since Pheasey Farms. It was a rare opportunity for old friends in the battalion who hadn't seen each other for a long time to get together and exchange experiences." +

The battalion left Bristol in companies over the week 24th to 30th June. Battalion H.Q. went first sailing across the channel and landing on Omaha Beach. Once the unit had been reunited it took up port duties in Cherbourg.

A large number of men who had been processed at Pheasey hit the Normandy beaches on June 6th.

Johnnie Alegrezza

Johnnie Alegrezza landed on Utah Beach on D-Day. Born in Shaw, Mississippi, Johnnie had arrived in Liverpool aboard the merchant ship, Cape Town Castle. From there he travelled by train to Pheasey where he spent four months. At the end of May he was assigned to E Company, 22nd Regiment, of the 4th Infantry Division. He was

**4th Replacement Battalion Archives.*
+*Unit History 769th M.P. Battalion.*

confined to camp for two weeks while he and his colleagues studied maps and models of the Normandy Beaches and surrounding countryside.

On June 4th the 4th Division boarded troopships although bad weather meant that there was two days wait before the invasion plan went ahead. Johnnie remembers crouching in a landing craft as he neared Utah Beach. One soldier attempted to jump over the side into the sea but the other men restrained him and the officer in charge threatened to shoot him if he did it again. Johnnie recalls the actual landing as a very frightening experience. He remembers seeing a large number of dead and wounded on the beach.

After moving inland from the beaches Johnnie was in continuous combat for ten days until he got wounded in his leg at Monetburg. He was returned to England where he spent seven months in hospital and convalescing, some of this time was spent at Pheasey.

At the beginning of 1945 Johnnie was returned to front line combat. At one point he and his outfit, who were all very hungry, came across a field of turnips near the German front lines. The men drew straws to see who should crawl into the field to collect the turnips. Unfortunately it was Johnnie who drew the short straw. As he crawled through the field he was shot at several times before being hit in the same leg that he had injured before.

This time Johnnie was hospitalised in England for one month and then sent back

Fred Petrogallo (F. Petrogallo)

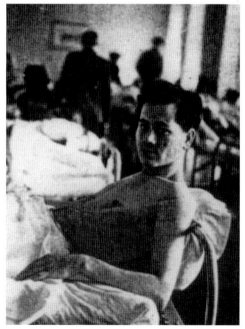

Johnnie Alegrezza in military hospital in southern England (M. Ditch)

to the United States for an honorable discharge. In 1999 Johnnie returned to the Normandy Beaches in France to visit the American Military Cemetery. He was saddened to find the graves of some of his friends that he had been split up from on Utah Beach. Some of them had come through Pheasey with him and up to this point he had not known their fate.

Pat Capasso

Pat Capasso also landed on Utah Beach on D-Day. Although he was assigned to the 101st Airborne Division he went over with the Invasion Force by boat. In the early hours of 4th June Pat and the rest of his group boarded troopships at Torquay. Pat recalls:

We weren't sure if it was for real or another drill."

Because of the bad weather the ships moved out of port on 5th June. Pat realised that it wasn't a drill when he passed a cruiser whose crew stopped to salute the troopship. In the early hours of 6th June Pat landed on Utah Beach, just 15 minutes after the first wave of troops. The Unit's mission was to secure a footing at the rear of the beach to site anti aircraft guns. Pat remembers the day vividly:

"As we approached the beach the noise was deafening with a continuous roar from a combination of planes, anti-aircraft fire, shelling and small arms fire."

As Pat (carrying a 50mm machine gun barrel) and his five man squad hit the beach they threw themselves into the nearest bomb crater.

Johnnie Alegrezza 1999 (M. Ditch)

"From the crater we slowly inched our way forward on our stomachs, crawling through barbed wires and jagged steel posts. I saw dead soldiers all around me and many injured being attended by medics. Ahead of us, in front of our objective, lay a German pillbox, which had already been hit by shells from our ships. There was a dent in the reinforced concrete. We didn't think anyone was still there but we didn't feel like taking any additional risks, so one of our guys tossed in a grenade, just to make sure.

"Eventually, after the best part of an hour we made it to the wall above the beach. That was the longest 200 yards I've seen or covered in my life. Once we were on the wall we set up the machine gun and filled sandbags to build a pit to protect it. All around I could see other guys of the 101st coming up to join us on the wall. Within an hour we had about twenty guns set up and firing at the German planes in order to protect our guys who were still coming ashore. All we wanted to do was to protect the rest of the invasion troops so they could move forward and get where they were supposed to go. We knew this invasion had to succeed if we wanted to get home.

"Throughout the remainder of the day we came under fire from the German 88mm. Guns and it was real scary. I had a prayer that my mother had written on a piece of paper which I kept in my jacket pocket. I read it through as we lay holed up and on subsequent occasions. I think that helped me through."

Following these events Pat and the other men of the 101st moved inland to join the rest of the unit. The 101st were involved in a number of campaigns including Operation Market Garden, The Battle of the Bulge and the Collmar Pocket. Pat was awarded a Bronze star for his role in the fighting in Belgium. Pat describes this time in his life as changing him:

"from a boy to being a man in short order."

**Land In Normandy;
Wounded 10th Day**

PFC. JOHNNY ALEGREZZA

Pfc. Johnny Alegrezza, son of Mr. and Mrs. Sante Alegrezza of Shaw, was among the first American troops to go ashore on the Normandy beach on "D" day, and fought for ten days before being wounded in the leg, which necessitated his removal to a hospital in England.

Johnny volunteered in the service in 1940 with his parents' consent, as he was only 16 years of age. He received his basic training at Fort Benning and August, Ga., and had been stationed in England months when the invasion was made. He was attached to Company E, 22nd Infantry Division.

Pfc. Alegrezza, in a recent letter to his sister, Mrs. Harry Love, formerly of Cleveland and now living in Greenville, stated he was getting along nicely, and would soon be able to be back in the fight.

JULY 27, 1944

News cutting Johnnie Alegrezza (M. Ditch)

Earl Lovelace

Earl Lovelace, who had been trained as a medical aide in America, was attached to the 2nd Infantry division after passing through Pheasey. He left Pheasey shortly before D-Day, travelling by truck and train to several high security areas where the men were inspected and issued with equipment.

The 2nd Division, which was attached to 5th Corps, 1st U.S. army, landed on Omaha Beach on D-Day plus one. Earl was a medic attached to M. Company, 38th Regiment. Once landed the 2nd Division pushed inland between the 1st and 29th Divisions, which had landed on the previous day. The 2nd's first objective was to take the city of Trevieres, which it achieved on 10th June.

Following this battle the Division was in continuous combat, taking Cersy, St.Germain d'Elles, and St. George d'Elle. It also took part in the Le Parc defensive and fought at Vire, Tinchebray and in the St. Lo area. The 2nd crossed the Rhine at Remagen and took part in the battle of Leipzig where Earl was injured in the hands and arms. As he was not badly wounded he treated himself and remained with his unit. In the latter days of the conflict the 2nd were attached to Patton's Third Army and were involved in liberating Pilsen in Germany.

Fred Petragallo

Fred Petragallo landed on Omaha Beach one day after Earl Lovelace. He had received his orders to move out of Pheasey Camp in January 1944 when he was assigned to 190th Field Artillery Battalion. In March the Battalion was alerted for combat. It moved to Bude, Cornwall, where the men were put through an artillery training programme. Every third week was spent on manoeuvres on Dartmoor.

On May 18th the Battalion left Bude for a marshalling area on the South coast of Cornwall which was code-named 'Sausage B'. On 1st June the men left for Falmouth where they loaded their equipment onto Landing Ship Tanks, which would carry the armoured vehicles to France. The men then boarded the ships where they were to spend the next six days. It took two days for the convoy to form. Seasickness pills were issued but due to a misunderstanding about the day the convoy would sail many men took them twelve hours before the boats even moved.

The convoy finally moved out to sea, and on 7th June the 190th and their equipment neared Omaha Beach. Fred remembers his first impressions of the scene:

"Off on the horizon we could see a cargo ship blazing and then slowly sink. This was the first sight of the war. We were worried and scared. Puffs of smoke came up from detonated mines and the low thud of exploding German shells could be heard."

The 190th were the first unit with 155mm. guns (nicknamed Long Toms) to land, and Fred remembers that some of the men of the 1st Infantry division, which the 190th were supporting, actually kissed the gun tubes as they were brought ashore.

By the time the 190th landed the fighting was a mile or two inland. The unit's first objective was to reach St. Laurent Sur Mer, a small Norman village on the coast of France. All of the men made it and the Battalion reunited at nearby Coleville Sur Mer where hand to hand fighting in the streets had just finished. From this time the men were engaged in the major battles through France, Belgium and Germany. At one point Fred remembers the Battalion being sent to Verdon to give General Patton and his Third Army artillery support.

By the end of July 1944 the 190th were in at the breakthrough at St.Lo in Operation Cobra. Their first fatal casualty was on 1st August when Private Harry Ream stood on a German mine. At LeChannon Edward G. Robinson visited the Battalion and became a temporary cannoneer.

After the battle at Vire some of the men spent a few days from August 18th to 24th at LeBisson for R. and R. Fred himself had no R. and R. during the war but remembers some brief lulls in the fighting before and after the 'Battle of the Bulge'. After V.E.Day Fred was lucky enough to win a lottery for a much appreciated seven day leave in Paris. After the Battle of Vire the Battalion was assigned to support the 4th U.S. Infantry Division, and on October 28th the men entered Germany.

On May 4th 1945 the 190th Field Artillery fired its 65,678th round, which was to be its last, at the village of Rybrik. While enroute to Cholesov, Czechoslovakia, on May 7th, the Battalion received orders to cease all firing and all movements. Czechoslovakia was the ninth European country that the Battalion had been stationed in since its Atlantic crossing.

John Carpenter

On 5th June John Carpenter was sent from Pheasey to Portsmouth where he was assigned to the 328th Harbour Craft Unit. The next day he remembers seeing the first batch of wounded returning from the French beaches for hospitalisation in England. This group consisted of English Commandoes and American Rangers.

The 328th were split into two sections, one group being assigned to tug boats, the other half to Liberty Ships. Rose Carpenter comments that:

"The reasoning behind splitting them up that way was that if one section got blown up they still had the other half to carry on."

John was assigned to a Liberty Ship,which he boarded on June 9th. This ship remained in the English Channel until the end of June when Cherbourg fell.

During this period it was necessary for the men to sleep on the top deck as the lower decks were full of supplies for the 'push' across France. There were no latrines on board so the soldiers had to climb over the side of the ship and use a rope and board arrangement. During the fortnight or so they were on board the men didn't shave so by the time they were ready to land they all had beards which they had to shave off using salt water so that their gas masks would fit, should they need them.

The Liberty ship was not able to land in Cherbourg Harbour because of the number of smaller craft, particularly landing barges, so it landed nearby and the men walked to the harbour where they were reunited with the other half of the unit which had landed the two tug boats.

John recalls being involved in several skirmishes while with the Harbour Craft Unit, but the most dramatic incident occurred when the ship that he was unloading was bombed. Fortunately he managed to escape before the ship sank.

CHAPTER 19
Stand and Wait

Tom Morissey was stationed at Pheasey Camp awaiting reassignment on June 6th 1944. He remembers:

"When the invasion was announced we were put on alert and all leave was cancelled. Helmets and arms appeared — - and a sobering attitude prevailed. Throughout all my life I've never gotten over the sombre mood of the camp personnel on that day. I was corporal of the guard and was also required to do a turn at sentry duty."

Over the next few days, members of the invasion forces who didn't make it to the beaches were brought to Pheasey and ordered to 'stand and wait'. Tom recalls:

"The returning survivors of that day are especially memorable to me. Some were recognisable by the American flag emblem shoulder patch they wore. Others, who ended up in the cold water of the channel, had a change of poor fitting clothing – they had a 'thrown together' look. Those soldiers were celebrities whether or not they sought to be. For the most part they were quiet, some had stories to tell. Eye witness accounts of the landing spread across the camp like wildfire."

Residents remember that the men evacuated from the water on D-Day were put up in tents on the Queslett Road. Edna Baker remembers that several wounded men were moved into billets at the lower end of Rippingille Road. She recalls that one, called Jim, sent for his English girlfriend to join him. Edna invited the young lady to stay with her for two or three weeks while Jim convalesced. Jim presumed that he would return to France when he recovered but his leg wound was more serious than he realised and he was sent home to America instead.

Not all of the soldiers who arrived at Pheasey from the D-Day landings survived to be sent home. Rachel Barton remembers seeing a group of medical personnel gathering around one such unfortunate G.I.

During marching and drill sessions Tom Morrissey became friendly with a tank driver whose amphibious tank went to the bottom of the channel in the rough swells (which were ten to twelve feet high) when the flotation collar malfunctioned. He and his crew watched the invasion from the sea, floating in a life jacket. Tom remembers that all the tank crew members he met had the same complaint – that the amphibious tanks were never tested in rough water and so when it came to using them in the channel they were ineffective.

Around this time Tom also became friendly with Vaughan Pierce:

"- - a handsome gentleman who, at 18, was drafted out of Carnegie Technical College in Pittsburg, P.A. where he majored in engineering and was two years shy of obtaining his degree. Had he been 21 his curriculum would have been completed and

would have merited him a direct commission upon entry into service. Instead after 'Basic Training' in the U.S. he was sent overseas to Pheasey Farms."

From Pheasey Tom and Vaughan were sent to Tidworth Barracks, Salisbury Plain, for combat training. Tom remembers:

"At Tidworth Vaughan occupied the upper of a double deck bed, I slept in the lower one. We were in the same rifle platoon but not in the same squad. From Tidworth we went to France. I learned of his death soon after a battle we were both involved in one afternoon in November 1944. I would have preferred not to know. I've thought of him so often throughout the war years and will remember him forever."

After D-Day the role of Pheasey and its parent station, Whittington, altered. They became 'Reinforcement Depots' as the men that were processed there were sent to 'reinforce' combat units on the front lines, which had become depleted due to casualties.

Both depots were very busy as they continued to process troops arriving from the States, but now also had the job of reprocessing troops arriving from the combat zone. The wounded and shell shocked stayed at Pheasey for a while, those who were deemed fit were reprocessed and returned to France within a short time. Those unfit for combat were repatriated back to America.

During July 1944 the 4th Reinforcement Battalion began handling 'packages'. The first package was shipped on 23rd of July by the 294th Reinforcement Company. It contained three hundred officers and enlisted men who had been equipped and armed so that they could be returned to their former units.

The soldiers who were given time for R. and R. at Pheasey made the most of their time before they were sent back into combat. One officer, who had been wounded while serving with one of the airborne units, remembers his time at Pheasey as ' the most agreeable time of his war'. He spent two months at the camp from July to September 1944. He remembers enjoying visiting the Perry Barr Dog Track, the Repertory Theatre and Princes Hotel where Allen Rock and his three piece ensemble played. Other evenings he spent waiting in line for fish and chips.

Bob Catlin arrived at Pheasey shortly before V.E. Day. He had been a rifleman in the 90th Division and had been in combat since 1st of November 1944. In his words he:

"Made out O.K. until we went into the Battle of the Bulge. The third day I got shrapnel in my right leg."

He was sent to a hospital at Metz and then to one in Cirencester. Once he had been discharged and taken a 7 day leave in Scotland he was sent to the 10th Replacement Depot for reassignment. As he had a family back in the States he hoped to be sent home, but from Pheasey he was reassigned to the 75th Infantry Division serving in France, where he was given duties in Special Service and with Prisoners of War.

As the war progressed men were sent to France to claim captured equipment. Large quantities of captured German equipment and aircraft were packed up by Air

Robert Catlin July 30th 1945 Attached to the 75th Division (R. Catlin)

Technical Intelligence and sent back to England and The United States via British Aircraft Carrier, H.M.S. Reaper. This procedure was known as 'Operation Lusty.'

Bill Rumold, the motor transport and maintenance officer at Pheasey, remembers:

"One evening in my motor pool two or three days after the American Army captured the city of Cherbourg, I glanced down the road and saw two large army trucks with semi-trailers wending their way up the road towards me in my humble motor officer's office. (16 foot by 16 foot wooden enclosed pyramidal tent frame.)"

The tractor trailer truck drove up to Bill and the driver explained the nature of their cargo:

"Each semi-trailer carried the major rotating element of electrical generators from the city of Cherbourg. The drivers had been ordered to take the two rotating elements (armatures) and ancillaries to the G.E.C. plant in Birmingham.

" I immediately made arrangements to feed and bed down the drivers and to escort them the following morning to the G.E.C. plant. So the following morning we delivered the two armatures, which had been sabotaged by the Germans,, to the G.E.C. I never saw the two drivers again and I never found out how long it took General Electric to repair the parts.

The twelve months following D-Day were busy for all of the reinforcement battalions based at Pheasey. 1st Lieutenant Martin T.Anderson, the historian for the 49th Reinforcement Battalion wrote that from D-Day to April 1945 the battalion:

"- - - processed and trained approximately 35,000 enlisted men, this number included reinforcements, casuals for shipment to combat and service units on the continent, limited assignment men for shipment to 70th A.A.F. depot Ground Force Training Centre and other units in addition to several hundred enlisted men to 12th Reinforcement Depot (Tidworth) for retraining for combat." [*]

During March 1945 the 321st, 322nd and 323rd Reinforcement Companies processed 2,464; 1,937; and 2,333 men respectively. The 4th Reinforcement Battalion was also responsible for processing a large number of G.I.s. During the twelve-month period following D-Day it shipped 204 packages.

"During the month of March 1945 the Battalion formed, equipped and shipped 35 Reinforcement Companies of 201 or 205 men each. This involved approximately 7,170 officers and enlisted men." [+]

In April 1945, towards the end of the war in Europe, two large bulletin boards were put up in each company area of the 4th Battalion so that the men could follow the progress of the final stages of the war.

---

[*] *History of the 49th Reinforcement Battalion.*
[+] *History of the 4th Reinforcement Battalion.*

CHAPTER 20

Gone, but not Forgotten

Moves were made to scale down the operations at Pheasey some time before V.E. Day. On 30th April 1945 the 4th Reinforcement Battalion were advised to prepare for a move. Equipment was measured, shipping crates made and individual clothing and equipment were marked. The kit bags of the assigned personnel were stencilled with the individual's name, rank, army service number, shipment number and appropriate code shipment marking. As a result the Battalion stood ready to depart at 24 hours notice if necessary.

On 8th May Major Francis Free, Commanding Officer of the 4th sent a memo to the Commanding General of the Ground Force Replacement Command:

"On 7th May 1945 at 1900 hours the Bn. Received notification that 8 May 1945 would be observed as V.E. Day. There was no change in the routine functioning of the Battalion during the V.E. holidays except that as many men as possible were given passes."*

Bob Catlin, who was on duty at Pheasey on V.E. Day remembers that most of the men at the base had passes and went into town, so the camp was very quiet. Bob had a pass for the following day and he remembers going into Birmingham:

VE Day Party on the Pheasey Estate (Glenys Pitt)

*History of the 4th Reinforcement Battalion.

"where the streets were full of people celebrating even then."

Bob was at the Pheasey for three weeks and this was the only time he had the opportunity to go off base.

There was no official party organised on the base for V.E. Day but residents on and around the estate held parties, which the Americans attended. Rosina Hart lived in Dyas Road. She remembers visiting the camp at Pheasey to ask the Commanding Officer if he was able to contribute anything towards the party in her road. On V.E. Day she arrived home from work to find two huge boxes filled with food in the middle of the street. Once the party was underway Rosina heard music. She looked up to see a marching band of G.I.s with trumpets and drums come around the corner. She recalls:

"It was absolutely fabulous and it made the children's day. It was such a wonderful gesture."

The soldiers lent various items such as flags and bunting to the residents for the street party in Moreland Road. Maxwell Coppock, a youngster at the time, remembers looking forward to the party but unfortunately he caught measles and had to watch the proceedings from his bedroom.

There was a huge bonfire on the corner of Crome Road and Tyndale Crescent. Pat Simmons attended the party there and remembers that it got so hot that it burnt a hole in the surface of the road. Terry Westwood also remembers seeing the large area of molten ash and tar the next day. Pat soon got warm dancing around the bonfire so she took off her navy blue reefer coat with a silk scarf attached to it. Unfortunately,

V.E. Day Party rear of Deer's Leap pub (B. Clewley)

VE Day Celebrations in Birmingham (Birmingham Evening Mail)

with everything else that was lying around, it got thrown on the bonfire. Pat remembers vividly the telling off and smack she got for losing her coat.

On 25th May the 293rd Reinforcement Company (4th Reinforcement Battalion) with four officers and 65 enlisted men moved from Pheasey to Whittington. The move took most of the day as only two trucks were used to shuttle the men between the two barracks. On 27th May the Headquarters and headquarters detachment with five officers and eleven enlisted men moved to Whittington. Again the move was carried out with the use of just two trucks. It started at 0930 hours and was completed by 1800 hours. On 31st May one officer and ten enlisted men of the 269th Reinforcement Company were moved to Whittington.

On 8th June Major Winston went to Raeburn Road School to say goodbye to the staff and children there. He donated a number of U.S. Army chairs and tables for the school's use. Later in the day the remaining four officers and 31 enlisted men of the 4th Battalion were moved by truck from Pheasey Farms to Whittington. On 9th June Pheasey Farms was closed as a subdepot of the 10th Reinforcement Depot. On 10th June the remaining men of the 49th Reinforcement Battalion were alerted for departure. They left Pheasey Farms on 10th July.

Roy Fleming remembers visiting the base with his father, as the G.I.s were packing up to leave. Mr Fleming kept twenty pigs and it was his usual custom to call in at the base to pick up the kitchen waste for use as pigswill. On arrival at the rear of the kitchens the Flemings were amazed to see a mountain of used army clothing heaped

Earl Lovelace and Jack Basso (E. Lovelace)

by the waste bins. Upon enquiry the Flemings were told that the G.I.s were getting rid of the 'heap', so Roy's father loaded up his truck with the entire stock, of which the majority of items were underwear and socks. Apparently it took Roy's mother two weeks to wash all the items that had been loaded into the lorry along with the pigswill. All of the male members of Roy's family were supplied with underwear as were the Fleming's friends. There was even some left over to be sent to a local charity.

The local residents were the grateful recipients of a number of items that the G.I.s couldn't take with them. Edna Baker remembers one of the cooks giving her a large parcel wrapped in an army towel. When she opened it she found the carcass of a sheep. Her next door neighbour cut it up for her so that it could be distributed amongst the rest of the neighbours.

While at Pheasey Earl Lovelace and Jack Basso had clubbed together to buy a bike. They agreed that when they left, they would give it to their friends, Olive and Roland White. Earl recalls:

"When that day came they were so grateful you would think it was an automobile."

He also remembers:

"When I left I asked Roland for his address and wrote it in my book. He told me it was 80, Raeburn Road. I wrote 8T. He looked at that and burst out laughing saying, It's not 8T, it's eighty!"

Another resident recalls that when the men left Pheasey they threw the wooden

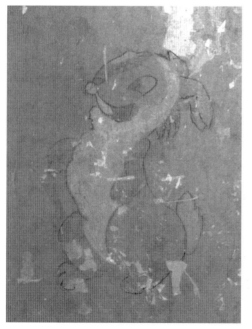 

Disney Characters found on the walls of Chantrey Crescent (J. Parkes)

bunks out of the window. He collected the wood and used it to build a garden shed for himself.

Maxwell Coppock remembers that as soon as the local residents realised that all of the G.I.s had left Pheasey they started ransacking the houses for any useful items that they could find. Maxwell recalls that his mother acquired a long handled broom and a folding metal bed. Later that day M.P.s in jeeps and trucks returned to the camp to put a stop to the looting. Maxwell recalls that his mother was terrified, as the M.P.s started calling at the civilian houses to search for military property. The residents had to return what they had taken although they suspected that the items would only be dumped.

Near the Trees bedding and other items were burnt on a bonfire. Howard Buckley remembers seeing a pile of furniture being made into a bonfire by the G.I.s. The Americans left before it was properly alight so the residents managed to pull some of the furniture out of the pile and rescue it.

The residents complained that furniture was being burnt while they had difficulty in obtaining items such as these with the rationing situation and shortages in Britain. They were told that it was not possible to donate the items to them as this would upset the local economy. This was a small consolation to people who saw the situation as causing senseless waste.

When the Americans left the First National Housing Trust was given the houses back, but they were now in quite a different state. Many of the banisters, and in some cases, the stairs, doors and floorboards, had been used for firewood. The American

Female forms on the wall at Chantrey Crescent (I. Bell)

The building of houses and amenities on the Pheasey Estate recommenced in 1946, This photo C.1950 (Walsall Local History Centre)

Government had to pay compensation because of the damage that had been done to the property.

Roland White was one of the plasterers who were called in to make the houses habitable again. He saw a number of pictures that the G.I.s had painted on to the walls in the houses to brighten up their drab surroundings. Several years later, residents found, and are still finding, paintings under the wallpaper when they decorate. Jean Bridgeman remembers finding a sketch of a Red Indian on the wall in her house when she and her husband stripped the wallpaper off. Bob Adams remembers seeing a painting of a South Sea Island on a wall in one of the houses while Terry Westwood remembers seeing a large Stars and Stripes flag in another. He recalls that it had been painted in oil paints and was almost impossible to move. One family tried everything they could to get rid of the painting in their house but no matter what they did each time they decorated, it showed through the wallpaper. In desperation the family had to replaster the walls in the room. Ron Crisp remembers that the local people were advised not to take any girls upstairs in the houses that had been used by the Americans, as some of the paintings were rather risque.

On September 13th 1945 the houses were put up for sale. By 4.a.m. there was a two mile long queue of people hoping to buy one of the 410 houses. The houses were priced at £500 - £575. A number of people changed their minds when they looked around the houses and saw the condition that they were in, some had no interior walls upstairs. Nevertheless the houses were in demand as the bombings during the war had

Tree donated to the school by Charles Hinde (M. Collins)

caused a housing shortage.

Keith Leighfield's parents were in the queue to buy a house on the estate. By the time they got to the front of the queue there was only one house left and the clerk told them to come back the next day when she would make a decision. As Mr. Leighfield left the clerk noticed that he was wearing the type of demob suit that indicated that he had been discharged from a military hospital. The clerk told the Leighfields that this would give the family priority and they were able to purchase 25, Chantrey Crescent.

Many of the houses were bought by families and therefore there was a sudden increase in the number of children of school age on the estate. This caused a problem to the Local Education Authority as the only school for the estate was Raeburn Road School, which consisted of a number of temporary wooden huts. After considerable negotiation the Community Centre was acquired and in 1946 a Junior Mixed School for 260 children was opened. Charles Hinde, a former G.I. who was billeted and worked in the Community Centre, donated money for a tree to be planted in the grounds of the school in memory of the American servicemen who were stationed there.

Collingwood Primary School was closed in 1993 and the building was refurbished in preparation to revert to its intended use as a Community Centre. On a snowy day in November 1996 the building was officially opened as a Community Centre by the Mayor of Walsall, Councillor Richard Worral and local councillor, Councillor Bill Newman. At the opening a wreath was laid and a plaque unveiled which was dedicated

Dedication Plaque, November 1996 (M. Collins)

Service of Dedication of the West Window,
AT THE GARRISON CHURCH OF SAINT GEORGE

Insignia of the 10th Replacement Depot
United States Army

Sunday April 30th 2000
Whittington Barracks, Lichfield

Wartime Home of the 10th American Replacement Division
1942-1945, who gave freely of their money for the stain glass of the West
Window. A window dedicated to the memory of their colleagues, who gave their
lives for the Freedoms depicted in it:

Freedom Of Speech, Freedom Of Religion, Freedom From Want, Freedom From Fear.

Programme from the service dedication Whittington Barracks, April 2000 (M. Collins)

British Legion, WWII military enthusiasts and WWII military vehicles on the parade ground at Whittington Barracks during the ceremonies for dedication of the window in the Garrison Chapel

Retired serviceman Frank Miller, left, who lives in Lichfield, Brian Goodman, from Tamworth, who staged the exhibition, and Lieutenant Colonel William Rumold, an American veteran from New Jersey

The Yanks are over here again – for major display

An American war veteran flew in from his home in New Jersey to take part in a show in Staffordshire

Retired Lieutenant Colonel William Rumold took part in the show The GIs are Back at the Staffordshire Regimental Museum, at Whittington Barracks, Tamworth Road.

Pictures: David Hamilton
Words: Alison Dayani

The event, which took place over the weekend and the Bank Holiday, focused on the 350,000 GIs who passed through the barracks between 1942 and 1944.

Memorabilia belonging to collector Brian Goodman was on display, and there was also a

parade of US military vehicles, re-enactments of famous battles, army recruitment displays, an abseiling tower, stalls, a bouncy castle and fair.

There was also music from the military bands of the Prince of Wales Division and the Volunteer Band of the Staffordshire Regiment, as well as a big band dance and disco and a 1940s-themed fancy dress competition.

News cutting from the Express and Star for the dedication day (Express and Star)
Insert: Old Stars and Stripes newspaper found at Chantrey Crescent (K. Colson)

to the servicemen who were stationed on the Pheasey Farms Estate during the war. The ceremony was attended by members of the British Legion, soldiers from the South Staffordshire Regiment, a U.S Colour Party from R.A.F. Mildenhall and members of the public.

In April 2000 a small number of G.I.s who had served at Whittington and Pheasey returned to their old haunts. They came to take part in the ceremonies to dedicate the stained glass window in the Garrison Church at Whittington Barracks. Apparently Americans who served at the 10th Replacement Depot donated money for the window during the war and it was installed in January 1945. Due to an oversight it was never dedicated. The G.I.s and their families who made the trip enjoyed the ceremony which included military marching bands and a flypast by a P51 Mustang. Brian Goodman, local military researcher, organised a display of World War Two Military vehicles, photos and memorabilia adjacent to the barracks wall, which was also appreciated by the G.I.s.

A visitor to Pheasey Farms Estate today would see few traces of its former use as an American Replacement Depot. In the Community Centre the square projection holes can be seen in the room which was used by the G.I.s as a cinema. Residents occasionally dig up items such as American badges and buttons in their garden and one man recently found an American Forces newspaper dated 25/5/44 lodged into the plasterwork of one of the interior walls of his house in Chantrey Crescent. A family who were carrying out some electrical rewiring in their house were surprised to find a number of beer bottles under the floorboards in one room, no doubt left by the house's former residents.

M. Collins with his 1943 Ford G.P.W. jeep outside
the Collingwood community centre, 1997 (R. Webb)

ABBREVIATIONS AND TERMS

A.P.O. – Army Post Office.

A.W.O.L. – Absent Without Leave.

B.P.O. – Base Post Office.

C.O. – Commanding Officer.

Comm. Z. – Communication Zone. – Area behind Combat Zone.

E.T.O. – European Theatre of Operations.

H.Q. – Headquarters.

K.P. – Kitchen Police.

M.P. – Military Police.

P.X. – Post Exchange – Equivalent of British Naafi.

P.T.O. – Pacific Theatre of Operations.

Q.M. – Quartermaster.

R .and R. – Rest and Recuperation – Given to combat weary soldiers.

S.O.S. – Services of Supply – Responsible for administrative supply and service activities of the War Department in the U.K. Also responsible for extending the communication and transportation systems to meet wartime demands.

T.D. (or T.D.Y.) – Temporary Duty.

W.A.A.C. – Women's Auxiliary Army Corps. – became -

W.A.C. – Women's Army Corps in 1943.

W.B.S. – Western Base Section. – Western part of U.K.

Assigned – having permanent duties at a station.

Unassigned – unattached to any station or unit, usually in the process of being assigned.

Attached – having temporary duties at a station.

Detached – detailed for Special Service. (D.S. – Detached Services)

Special Service – Education and entertainment section.

Package – Group of soldiers sent from a Replacement Depot to a combat unit.

APPENDIX 1: LIST OF REPLACEMENT DEPOTS IN U.K.

Replacement/Reinforcement Depots.

1st – Llandaff, Wales.

2nd – Cheltenham / Bristol, Gloucestershire.

3rd – Bangor, Northern Ireland / Yeovil, Somerset.

4th – Oulton Park, Cheshire.

5th – Castle Dawson, Northern Ireland.

6th – Coleraine, Londonderry, Northern Ireland.

7th – Dogleap, Londonderry, Northern Ireland.

8th – Bangor, Northern Ireland.

9th – Midsummer Norton, Somerset.

10th – Whittington, Lichfield, Staffordshire.

11th – Dogleap, Londonderry, Northern Ireland.

12th – Tidworth, Salisbury Plain, Wiltshire.

14th – Oulton Park, Cheshire.

16th – Coleraine, Londonderry / Warminster, Somerset.

17th – Yeovil, Somerset.

18th – Wollacombe, Devon / Landaff, Glamorgan.

19th – Oulton Park, Cheshire.

Detachments of the 10th Replacement Depot – Casual Pools –1944.

Det. B. and O. – Kirkby, Lancashire.

Det. C. – Simonswood, Lancashire.

Det. D. – Bristol, Somerset.

Det. F. – Salisbury, Wiltshire.

Det. G. – Belfast, Northern Ireland.

Det. L. – Glasgow, Scotland.

Det. R. – Barry, Glamorganshire.

Det. W. – Sudbury, Derbyshire.

Det. Z. – Cheltenham, Gloucestershire.

APPENDIX 2: LOCATION OF FIELD FORCE REPLACEMENT DEPOTS

APPENDIX 3: RANK BADGES

Officer's Rank Badges

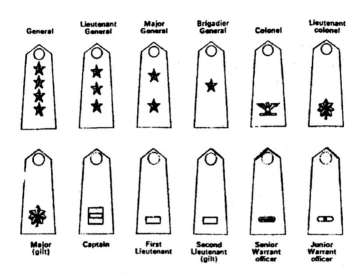

Enlisted Men's Rank Badges

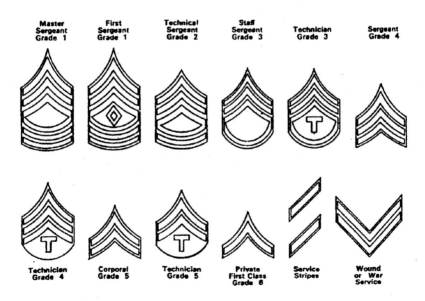

APPENDIX 4: ABREVIATED RANKS

Gen.	General
Col.	Colonel
Lt.	Col. Lieutenant Colonel
Maj.	Major
Capt.	Captain
1st Lt.	First Lieutenant
2nd Lt.	Second Lieutenant
C.W.O.	Chief (Senior) Warrant Officer
W.O.J.G.	Warrant Officer Junior Grade
Sgt.	Sergeant
Tech.Sgt.	Technical Sergeant
Tech.4.	Technical Grade 4
Cpl.	Corporal
Pfc.	Private First Class
Pvt.	Private